MUFFINS

Over 200 recipes
and variations
to accompany any meal

MUFFINS

Over 200 recipes and variations to accompany any meal

Francesca DiPaolo

Adams Media Corporation
Avon, Massachusetts

Published by
Adams Media Corporation
57 Littlefield Street, Avon, MA 02322. U.S.A.
www.adamsmedia.com

ISBN: 1-58062-252-6

Printed in Canada.

J I H G F E D C B

Library of Congress Cataloging-in-Publication
data available upon request from the publisher.

This publication is designed to provide accurate and authoritative information with
regard to the subject matter covered. It is sold with the understanding that the
publisher is not engaged in rendering legal, accounting, or other professional advice.
If legal advice or other expert assistance is required, the services of a competent
professional person should be sought.
— From a Declaration of Principles jointly adopted by a Committee
of the American Bar Association and a Committee of Publishers and Associations

Cover photo illustration by Will Nelson/Sweet Represents

This book is available at quantity discounts for bulk purchases.
For information, call 1-800-872-5627

This book is dedicated to the memory of my aunt,
Nunziata ("Zia") DiPaolo

Beauty, Strength, Courage
She had it all—and so much more.

Contents

Acknowledgements

To my mother, Jennie, with love.

To Berit and Rich Michalson, and their family for the joy of friendship.

Many thanks to everyone at Pinder Lane & Garon-Brooke Associates for your support and generosity.

A special thank you to Jean Free, for your early interest in and enthusiasm for my manuscript.

A special thank you also to Bob Thixton, whose efforts and expertise made this book a reality.

Introduction

Muffin . . . connected with old French moufflet, soft, said of bread. (*The Oxford English Dictionary*)

Originating in northern England, muffins are among the most famous of English specialties. Although muffins must be of considerably earlier origin, recipes do not appear in published cookery books much before the eighteenth century. Muffins reached the zenith of their popularity in the nineteenth century and were traditionally eaten around an open fire at teatime. Made from a leavened batter of flour, milk, and butter, muffins were cooked on a griddle and served toasted, split and buttered. They were originally baked in town ovens and carried on a tray balanced on the head of the "muffin man" who rang a bell to tell customers of his imminent arrival. At one time, so many muffins were made that violence regularly broke out between rival sellers looking for trade.

This collection is a tribute to the diversity of muffins thriving in our contemporary culture. They're simple, humble, and perfectly scrumptious. Muffins as we know them appeared after the development of baking powder in the 1840s. Charming us ever since, muffins have made their way to our table again and again. Ours is a continuing love affair with their flavor, style, and simplicity.

A lively volume, *MUFFINS* takes a spirited new look at traditional favorites and offers luscious new temptations that will enchant your palate as they nourish your soul. These are the muffins that have many people rediscovering the pure, simple pleasures of home baking. And no wonder, few things can match the incomparable taste and heady aroma, or the satisfaction of turning out, from scratch, the sumptuous muffins that are so much a part of our rich culinary heritage and our ongoing baking traditions.

Most cooks think of muffins merely as breakfast or brunch fare. Yet, with a wide variety of fresh, wholesome ingredients and dozens of serving ideas to explore, you'll find muffins are, quite literally, the most versatile bread for every meal and occasion. They are remarkably easy to make and even easier to enjoy. Here are a few ideas to inspire your own delicious creations.

- Muffins earn their keep in picnic baskets or backpacks, at barbecues, while camping, or on weekend road trips. Portable and compact, they travel well and sustain travelers in style.

- Adding new variety to your menus, fresh-from-the-oven muffins offer a delicious change of pace from ordinary bread. If you like, bake a muffin batter as a quick bread loaf. Then slice the loaf and use it for sandwiches.

- Pack muffins for lunches to take to school or work.

- Try them for parties and buffets, brunches and teas.

- Muffins make beautiful gift baskets. Fill a wicker basket with an assortment of fresh-baked muffins, individually wrapped and labeled. Add cheeses, dessert sauces, flavored butters and honeys, or jams and preserves, along with tins of fine tea or coffee. Include a 2-cup pottery teapot and linen napkins if you wish. Wrap the entire basket with tinted cellophane and tie it with a festive ribbon. A great gift for friends or family, to welcome a new neighbor, or as a special thank you for a holiday host.

- Muffins travel very well. They make the ultimate comfort-food care package for anyone who lives abroad, is away at college, is spending a summer at camp, or is leaving home for the first time. And keep them in mind for great I-miss-you gifts, holiday presents, and birthday greetings.

- During the busy holiday season, plan ahead for "drop-in" visits. Muffins can be baked fresh and kept frozen, ready to reheat and serve when unexpected guests arrive. They add a festive dimension to any holiday table.

- Whether it's for a midmorning coffee break or to satisfy those after-school hunger pangs or late-night munchies, muffins are the perfect indulgence.

- Is it your turn to bring treats to the office or classroom? Muffins are always a favorite.

- Muffins are ideal for using leftovers to good advantage, for making small amounts of ingredients go further, and for providing a delicious solution to an overflowing garden.

From the main course through dessert, you'll find sweet and savory recipes to whet your appetite, and grace your table from breakfast to brunch to dinner. The variety of recipes will satisfy even the most insatiable muffin lover. These gems are not too rich or elaborate; instead, they're packed generously with flavor, texture, and style. *MUFFINS* features over two hundred delectable, sometimes surprising, but always perfect, recipes, including: Amaretto Walnut, Artichoke Cheddar, Banana Rum Raisin, Blue Cheese Cornmeal, Cornmeal Sausage, Fig and Smoked Ham, Macaroni and Cheese, Marbled Chocolate Cheesecake, Pizza, Pumpkin Curry, Raspberry Banana, Rum Eggnog, Smoked Turkey and Wild Rice, Spiced Mandarin Orange, Sun-Dried Tomato and Cheese, Sweet Potato–Maple Walnut, Tropical Papaya Spice, Tuna Muenster Melt, and Zucchini Ricotta.

There is something for everyone—for every taste, every mood, and every meal. With lots of tips to accompany the recipes, the homemade goodness of these muffins is yours in a snap. Happy baking!

Chapter 1

Ingredients

The ingredients I work with are straightforward; most everything can be purchased in a well-stocked supermarket. But just in case, I've also included mail-order sources for ingredients that may not be readily available in your area (see Appendix 2). Choose fresh, high-quality ingredients. They are essential for the best results. You can't do first-rate work with second-rate ingredients. Remember to protect staples from heat and light. Store flour, sugar, and other dry ingredients in canisters or jars with tight lids. If you are in doubt about the freshness of an ingredient, throw it away.

Baking Powder

This is double-acting baking powder. Keep it sealed tightly and store it in a cool, dry place.

Baking Soda

Baking soda is often used on its own to leaven batters that include acidic ingredients such as buttermilk, yogurt, citrus juices, sour milk, molasses, or honey. This combination gives one of the very tenderest crumbs.

Brown Sugar

Brown sugar is granulated sugar combined with molasses in varying quantities to yield light or dark varieties. Brown sugar is always measured in "packed" cups. Firmly press it into a dry-ingredient measuring cup, then level off the excess. Do not substitute "brownulated" or liquid-type sugar. To keep brown sugar soft, add a strip of orange peel to the box and store it tightly closed in the refrigerator. If you've purchased brown sugar that has become hard or lumpy, you can dissolve it into the recipe's ingredients to prevent lumps in your muffins.

Butter

I've used pure, sweet (unsalted) butter exclusively in all my testing. For tender-

ness, volume, and texture, no butter substitute measures up to the rich, delicate flavor of the real thing. Butter is always in sticks. Don't substitute whipped butter, liquid, blends, or tub spreads. They contain more water and less fat than the sticks; and although they may be better for you on the dinner table, they do not make for better muffins, or for better baking in general. To soften butter, bring it to a cool room temperature before baking. Pushing your finger into properly softened butter will leave a dent, but the butter will remain slightly firm. Stored in the freezer, butter will keep for months until needed. Tightly wrap butter to avoid exposure to air, since it easily absorbs the tastes and odors of other foods.

Buttermilk

Buttermilk contributes a tangy flavor and thick, creamy texture to muffins and baked goods. Its acidity increases the power of leavening agents like baking soda, thus adding extra lightness to batters. This is also true of sour cream.

Carob

Also known as St. John's bread, carob has a rich brown color and a delicate sweetness that suggests mild milk chocolate. It may be used in place of cocoa and chocolate. Carob brings a delicious, naturally sweet flavor to the recipe, while subtly boosting the calcium level of baked goods with its own calcium content. It contains no caffeine. You can buy unsweetened carob in chips or in powder that is either raw or roasted. Roasting brings out its full, rich flavor. Carob is sold in most natural food stores and in many supermarkets. Store it in a tightly covered container in a cool, dry place. To adapt a recipe that calls for chocolate, substitute carob powder measure for measure. As a substitute for 1 square of chocolate, use 3 level tablespoons of carob powder plus 2 tablespoons of milk or water.

Cheese

You can be quite flexible with the recipes for cheese-based muffins. Cheddar, Monterey Jack, parmesan, Swiss, Fontina, mozzarella, and Muenster are just a few of the many wonderful cheeses you can try, including smoked varieties. Most cheeses should be wrapped in moisture-proof, airtight wrappers. "Moldy" cheese like blue cheese are the one exception. These cheeses need to breathe and should be kept in covered containers, with slightly loosened tops.

Remember, too, that all cheeses keep best stored on the bottom shelf of the refrigerator. Shred, grate, or crumble 4 ounces of cheese for every cup of cheese called for in a recipe. The very hard cheeses are excellent for fine grating; the softer ones work best when shredded. Trying to grate a soft cheese too finely will only clog the grater. For easiest grating and shredding, use cheeses that are very cold.

Chili Peppers

Chili peppers are the unripened form of a wide variety of fresh peppers. As a seasoning, these peppers are dear to the hearts of many people (including me) and range from mild to hot. The green chilies used in these recipes are poblano, Anaheim, and jalapeño. Feel free to try any of your favorite chili peppers—just adjust the amount to your taste. For convenience, you can buy canned green chilies that are already roasted, peeled, and diced.

Chocolate

I tested the recipes calling for chocolate using Baker's baking chocolate. To melt chocolate without scorching, place it in a double boiler and simmer on a low heat.

Cocoa

Always use a better quality cocoa in baking. I use Hershey's unsweetened cocoa powder. Another cocoa you might want to try is Droste. Both are excellent and widely available. Do not use sweetened cocoas or hot chocolate mixes in place of pure cocoa powder. In these recipes you can either sift cocoa into the dry ingredients or blend it in with the liquid ingredients. Both methods work well.

Coconut

Coconut is the white, sweet meat of the fresh coconut. Ready-to-use forms are available in cans or plastic bags. Flaked coconut (the longer and moister pieces) or shredded coconut (the shorter and drier pieces) can be used interchangeably in recipes unless otherwise specified.

Coffee

Coffee is one of the best flavors used in baking. Recipes call for instant coffee or espresso powder (not freeze-dried crystals). Two excellent brands are Medaglia D'Oro and Café Salvador.

Cornmeal

A granular flour ground from dried kernels of yellow, blue, or white corn, cornmeal has a sweet, robust flavor. The commercial variety is available in fine or coarser grinds. Stone-ground cornmeal is made from whole corn kernels, and produces a richer flour.

Dried Fruit

Dried fruits are intensely flavored and satisfyingly chewy. Select ones with a softer texture. Some of the most succulent choices include apples, apricots, cherries, cranberries, currants, dates, figs (Calimyrna or Black Mission), peaches, pears, prunes, and raisins. Although the recipes specify one or another type of dried fruit, they are basically interchangeable. Dried fruit that has become dry or tough can be plumped up by covering it with boiling water and putting it in the refrigerator overnight. This doesn't cook the fruit. You can also plump raisins by simmering them in port rum or sherry. If you have a congealed mass of raisins, heat them in the oven at 300°F for a few minutes and they will unstick themselves.

Eggs

Eggs add a portion of the liquid requirement of the recipe and also provide some of the flavor. In addition, the baking process cooks the protein, which acts to support or stiffen the flour and keep the muffin from collapsing. Beating eggs mixes air into the liquid. When the muffin is heated in the oven, the air expands and leavens or lightens the muffins, thus helping them rise. I tested these recipes using large eggs. Buy the freshest ones available. If you are uncertain of the quality, test for freshness by lowering raw eggs into water. If they float, air pockets have formed under the shell and they are old. Before baking, bring eggs to room temperature by allowing them to stand 30 minutes to 1 hour.

Extracts

Always use pure flavor extracts.

Flour

All-purpose unbleached flour is used throughout this book unless otherwise specified. Do not use self-rising flour, which contains baking powder and salt, unless otherwise indicated. All-purpose flour, even with its long shelf life, must be stored in a dry, dark, moderately cool place. Stick a couple of bay leaves in the canister or bag to discourage "visitors." Whole-wheat and stone-ground flours are put in airtight plastic bags or containers and must be stored in the freezer or refrigerator to protect the essential oils that have not been processed out of the flour. They will keep up to three months. There are a wide variety of flours, including amaranth, quinoa, triticale, brown-rice, buckwheat, millet, oat, rye, barley, graham (low-gluten, "soft" whole-wheat flour), and semolina. Flour varies in the amount of moisture it contains, depending on day-to-day environmental humidity, conditions of storage, type of flour used, and elevation above sea level. Flour will be less subject to changes in humidity if it is stored in a glass jar with a wide mouth.

Honey

Honey lends moisture and a distinctive mellow sweetness to baked goods. Honeys with the lightest texture—thyme, orange blossom, clover, tupelo, and alfalfa—have the mildest flavor. Buckwheat, the darkest honey commonly available, is the most nutritious, but it can overpower the flavor of the muffins. Honey is stored, covered, at room temperature. If it becomes crystallized, you can easily reliquefy it by setting the jar in a pan of very hot water. Heating honey over 160°F, however, adversely affects the flavor.

Maple Syrup

Look for 100 percent pure maple syrup. It has a rich savor and intense sweetness. Do not use maple-flavored syrups. They are blends that contain as little as 2 percent maple syrup.

Molasses

Molasses is a thick, robust-tasting, syrupy by-product of sugarcane refining. Lighter grade, unsulphured molasses, which results from the first boiling of the syrup, works best in baking. The darkest syrup coming from the final boiling stage, called blackstrap molasses, is not recommended.

Nuts

Nuts like almonds, hazelnuts, peanuts, pecans, pistachios, walnuts, and macadamias add wonderful flavor and texture, and can be used interchangeably in these recipes. To ensure crunchiness, do not add nuts to the liquid part of the recipe (oil, milk, eggs), or they will soak up the liquid and become soggy. Buy nuts whole or in large pieces for the greatest freshness. To chop nuts, spread them in a single layer on a nonslip cutting surface. Using a chef's knife, carefully chop the nuts with a rocking motion of the blade. Avoid using blenders and food processors, because they tend to press out the oils and produce a pasty, rather than crunchy, grind. However, if this is the method you choose, grind nuts with some of the sugar from the recipe so they will not become oily and stick together. Store all nuts, whole or chopped, in an airtight container in the freezer, where they will keep for several months. At warm temperatures, their high oil content can quickly turn rancid. Do not buy nuts that are already toasted—they may be stale or even rancid. Nothing compares to freshly roasted nuts to bring out the richest flavor. Seeds also make great additions. Try poppy, sesame, sunflower, and pumpkin.

Note: Children often have life-threatening allergic reactions to nuts. Many of these muffin recipes include nuts in the ingredients. Nuts can be eliminated in every instance without harm to the recipe.

Oils

Because oil is not generally interchangeable with butter in baking, I have not used it in these recipes. One of its failings is that it is inclined to collect instead of remaining uniformly distributed throughout the batter. Baked goods will tend to be grainy, lacking the fluffy, moist texture and the creamy taste that butter provides.

Rolled Oats

Use regular oatmeal rather than quick-cooking or instant. It adds a grainy texture and nutlike taste to baked goods.

Shortening

For muffins that are flaky and tender, recipes were tested with Crisco solid vegetable shortening. Shortening may occasionally replace the butter content of a recipe. You may substitute regular or butter-flavored shortening in an equal amount to the butter required. Shortening is not a pure oil, nor is butter. Both contain about equal amounts of water and that is why equal amounts can be substituted. Lard is a poor substitute for shortening. Regular and diet margarines are not made for baking and should never be substituted for shortening or butter.

Sugar

Granulated sugar is used in most of the recipes, unless otherwise stated. Sugar substitutes should not be used. As a rule they do not provide the mass and structure of sugar and will not work. You will need to use recipes specifically designed for sugar substitutes.

Sun-Dried Tomatoes

These tomatoes have an intense, sweet-tart flavor and a slightly chewy texture. They are available either packed in oil or dry. Oil-packed tomatoes should be drained well before using.

Wheat Bran

This is unprocessed miller's wheat bran. Included in batter mixtures, bran lends robust flavor, texture, and a generous measure of dietary fiber. Oat and rice brans are also great sources of fiber and have a sweet nutty flavor. The recipes may be made with whichever bran you prefer. Store bran in the refrigerator or freezer.

Wheat Germ

Sold either raw or toasted, wheat germ adds a wholesome, nutlike taste and slightly crunchy texture to baked goods. Keep it stored in the refrigerator or in the freezer to prevent it from turning rancid. Wheat germ may be used directly from the freezer, where it will stay fresher longer.

Winter Squash

Winter squashes, like acorn, Golden Delicious, turban, butternut, Hubbard, or pumpkin, are delicious in muffins and quick breads. They can be found in the markets from fall to early spring. The squash must be cooked and mashed before using it in recipes. To prepare squash, cut it in half with a heavy, sharp kitchen knife. If the skin is very hard, use a mallet to tap the knife carefully once it is securely wedged in the squash.

Remove all seeds and fibers from each half. Place the squash halves, cut sides down, in a shallow baking dish. Bake in a 350°F oven until the squash is tender and the pulp begins to fall apart, 45 minutes to 1 hour or more, depending on size. Cool a few minutes for easier handling. Scrape the pulp from the shell, and mash it with a fork until smooth.

Zest

The outer rind of oranges and lemons, zest contains the citrus fruit's aromatic essential oils. It is a lively source of flavor in baking.

Chapter 2

Baking Utensils

Using the proper tools will simplify baking. They enable you to do things more easily and more accurately. They speed up mixing and help you achieve uniformly successful results. Make sure that all the utensils are clean.

Blender

Use a blender for making purées.

Chef's Knife

Select a knife with a good quality stainless-steel blade for general slicing, cutting, and chopping of ingredients.

Dry Measuring Cups

You'll need them in graduated sizes, for accurate measuring of dry ingredients.

Grater

Choose a grater with a sturdy, stainless-steel grating surface. Look for a four- to six-sided grater.

Kitchen Shears

Keep a pair of shears handy for cutting dried fruits. When cutting dried fruits, dip the blade into cold water to prevent sticking, or coat the blade with a nonstick vegetable spray.

Kitchen Timer

A timer is a must to prevent overcooking.

Loaf Pans

To bake quick breads, you may use either a large loaf pan (9 x 5 x 3 in., holds 8 cups), a medium pan (8½ x 4½ x 2½ in., holds 6 cups), or a miniature pan (6 x 3 x 2 inches, holds 2 cups). To make different loaf shapes, try a round springform pan, a square cake pan, a bundt pan, or a tube pan.

Measuring Spoons

Select metal spoons in graduated sizes with deep bowls.

Mixing Bowls

Choose high-sided, deep bowls for easier mixing. A large bowl holds dry ingredients. Use a medium bowl, with a lip for pouring, for liquid ingredients.

Muffin Tins

Recipes are written for a standard 12-cup, 3-inch muffin pan. Choose a heavy steel pan, because the bottom will diffuse heat more evenly. Lightweight pans may cause the crust to brown before the middle is done. All muffin pans, including the nonstick ones, require greasing. When using paper muffin cups, ignore the greasing step. If you use mini or jumbo muffin tins, you need to adjust the baking time accordingly. Read the manufacturer's suggestions for baking times, and be sure to test for doneness. A standard recipe for 1 dozen muffins makes about 3 dozen mini-muffins and requires approximately 10 to 15 minutes' baking time. A standard recipe for one dozen muffins makes about 6 jumbo muffins and requires approximately 20 to 30 minutes' baking time. Muffin tins and loaf pans also come in a variety of shapes. Muffins can be baked as fancy scallops, hearts, whimsical animals, and more.

Season all new baking pans by applying a very thin coat of vegetable oil and baking the empty pan for about 25 minutes at 400°F. Cool the pan completely, wipe it dry, and lightly grease it with all-purpose shortening before using.

Oven Thermometer

Regularly check your oven for accuracy with a good oven thermometer. Place it on the center rack and use the temperature it registers as your guide to adjusting the heat. Temperatures vary—400°F in one oven may actually be 375°F in another. You may have to adjust baking times somewhat. Oven thermometers are inexpensive and come in two types. One kind is used to measure the temperature of the baking item and the other kind is to measure the temperature of the oven. It is a good idea to use both types.

Paper Muffin Cups

Use paper cups made for jumbo muffin tins. They hold and shape the muffin batter better than the standard-size cups.

Rubber Spatula

You'll need a rubber spatula to scrape batters out of mixing bowls and to smooth the surfaces of batters in loaf pans.

Spouted Liquid Measuring Cup

Be sure to get one that is marked off in quarters and thirds for accurate measuring of liquid ingredients. Choose heavy-duty, heat-resistant glass.

Wire Cooling Rack

Wire racks allow air to circulate under baked muffins and loaves for quick, even cooling. Choose racks with closely spaced wires.

Wire Strainer, Medium (8 in.)

For sifting dry ingredients, a strainer does a better job than a sifter and is easier to use. It also shakes out, cleans, and stores more easily than a sifter.

Wire Whisk

Use a wire whisk to beat eggs or blend liquids before incorporating them into batters.

Wooden Spoon

This is essential for mixing batters.

Zester

Use it to cut citrus zest into fine shreds.

Chapter 3

Baking Hints and Tips

Accurate measuring of ingredients is a baking **must**; even the slightest difference in amounts can affect the recipe. If the recipe tells you to sift the flour—do it.

- To measure dry ingredients like flour or sugar, spoon the ingredient lightly into the measuring cup (never pack it down). Using the straight edge of a knife, level it out by scraping off the excess. Never shake or tap the measuring cup against the counter to even the amount. This will compact the ingredient and result in an inaccurate measure. Dry and powdered ingredients such as baking powder, baking soda, and spices are measured with measuring spoons. Fill the spoons to overflowing, then level as described here. Never use a liquid cup for measuring dry ingredients.

- To measure liquid ingredients, pour the liquid to the exact marking. Determine the accuracy by putting the cup on a level surface and viewing it at eye level. Always look at the measure at eye level. If it is seen from above, the appearance of the liquid's level will be distorted.

- Have butter, milk, and eggs at room temperature. If you're baking on the spur of the moment or you forgot to remove the eggs from the refrigerator in advance, remove the chill from the cold eggs by submerging them (in their shells) in a bowl of warm water for 10 minutes before using.

Baking soda and double-acting baking powder are both leavening agents, but they cannot be used interchangeably.

Baking soda (bicarbonate of soda) leavens dough by releasing carbon dioxide when it is mixed with an acidic liquid such as yogurt, buttermilk, or vinegar. As soon as baking soda comes into contact with the liquid, it starts to work. Baking soda should be stored in a cool, dry place away from strong odors.

Double-acting baking powder is a combination of baking soda, an acid like cream of tartar, and a starch like cornstarch or flour. It is called double-acting because its leaveners work in two stages: first, when it is mixed with a liquid; and again, when it is exposed to heat. Double-acting baking powder should be stored in the same manner as baking soda, but it has a limited shelf life and should be replaced frequently. Check the expiration date. It's often helpful to mark the date on the container when it's opened. Stale baking powder can ruin whatever you're making, but old powder isn't necessarily stale. To determine whether you need a fresh supply, pour 1 cup hot tap water over 1 teaspoon baking powder. The fresher the baking powder, the more actively the mixture will bubble. If the reaction is weak or does not occur, throw out the baking powder.

- Leftover buttermilk freezes beautifully and will last up to 3 months in the freezer. To reuse it, thaw the milk overnight in the refrigerator. Before using it, stir the buttermilk vigorously, as it will separate, and allow it to warm to room temperature.

- A common substitute for buttermilk is 1 cup milk blended with 2 tablespoons lemon juice or distilled white vinegar. Let the mixture stand for about 5 minutes or until it curdles. Another substitute may be made by combining 1 cup milk with 1¾ tablespoons cream of tartar.

- You can make your own brown sugar by adding ¼ cup molasses to ¾ cup granulated sugar. Mix thoroughly. This makes 1 cup firmly packed brown sugar.

- To toast nuts or sunflower, sesame, or pumpkin seeds, spread them in a single layer on an ungreased baking sheet and bake in a preheated oven. Shake the pan once or twice. Be sure to watch them closely because they burn easily. Toast seeds at 350°F for about 5 minutes, and almonds and hazelnuts at 350°F for 10 minutes. Toast more delicate walnuts and pecans very lightly at 325°F for 10 to 15 minutes, and extremely delicate macadamias at 300°F for about 10 minutes, until they barely color. If a recipe calls for chopped toasted nuts, toast the nuts whole and chop them afterward. Toasted nuts can be stored in the freezer, well wrapped, for several months. Nuts and seeds can also be toasted in a dry skillet on top of the stove using moderate heat.

- It's always convenient to have a fresh supply of citrus peel on hand. Whenever you use an orange, lemon, or grapefruit, wash it thoroughly with a stiff brush, then dry it. Using a vegetable peeler, peel off the colored top layer of skin in thin strips, taking care not to remove any white pith with it. Wrap the skin in paper toweling and place it in a warm spot to dry. After the peel dries, store it in the freezer, then grate it, slice it thinly, or chop it as needed. If you own a flat fine-tooth grater with one-sized hole, lay it directly over the bowl and grate the citrus peel right into the liquid ingredients so none of the essential oils and zest are lost. You can also use a zester. Draw across the fruit's skin, the zester removes the peel in thin strips.

- Packaged, shredded coconut will keep for 6 to 12 months unopened in your pantry. Once opened, it can be stored in the refrigerator for up to a month or in the freezer for a year. To toast coconut in the microwave, spread it thinly on a paper plate or towel and use the high setting for 2 or 3 minutes. Watch closely because the coconut will brown quickly.

- For an easy cleanup when using a metal grater to shred cheese, brush a thin coat of vegetable oil on the grater before you use it, or coat it lightly with a vegetable spray.

- Be sure your herbs and spices are fresh. It is best to purchase them in small quantities because their flavors diminish rapidly after opening. Tired herbs and spices produce tired-tasting muffins. The spices used here are ground (not whole), unless the recipe specifies differently.

- It is best to add chocolate chips, nuts, and cut-up dried fruits to the sifted dry ingredients. Stir the mixture to separate the pieces and coat them thoroughly. This prevents the pieces from settling to the bottom of the pan.

- Do not make substitutions unless the recipe specifies differently. Substitutions affect the moisture-to-flour balance.

Adding too much or too little of an ingredient throws this balance off. This may result in muffins that are soggy or dry, do not rise properly, or have other unwanted characteristics. If you do substitute an ingredient, use an ingredient that is like what the recipe calls for in texture and density, and keep in mind that twice as much isn't necessarily twice as good. **Don't double the recipe.**

Dip a sugar cube briefly in a liqueur, whiskey, or rum, and place it on top of the muffins before baking. This adds a wonderful touch to dessert muffins and to many fruit and vegetable muffins.

Measuring sweet syrups like honey, molasses, and maple syrup can be sticky and messy. Using a vegetable spray, lightly coat a glass measuring cup first, then pour the sweet syrup into the cup just to the level line. The syrup will pour out clean and easy.

Some of the recipes call for liqueurs. Don't substitute a fruit juice for a liqueur unless it is suggested in the recipe. The acids in the juice affect the action of the leaveners in the muffin batter.

Many types of muffins ship well. Cool them thoroughly and place them in plastic bags. Pack with plenty of popcorn (plastic or real) around them.

Chocolate scorches easily and must be melted with care over very low heat. A microwave works well. On the stove burner, use very low heat and melt the chocolate in a thick-bottomed pan, stirring constantly. You can also melt chocolate in a hot-water bath by placing a bowl holding the chocolate in a large saucepan filled with about 2 inches of water. The chocolate should be stirred while melting. Or melt chocolate in your oven by placing it in a cake baking pan and using very low heat (200° to 250°F). Remove it from the oven as soon as the chocolate is soft.

All your utensils for melting chocolate must be dry. If even a few drops of moisture get into the chocolate, it will become grainy and stiff. Stir in 1 teaspoon of oil to 2 ounces of chocolate to bring it back to its correct consistency.

Unsweetened chocolate will change into a liquid when melting. Semisweet chocolate and sweet chocolate will hold their shape until stirred.

Chocolate will stay fresh for about a year if it is stored between 65° and 70°F in a cool, dry place. When chocolate is stored at higher temperatures for a long time, cocoa butter comes to the surface and forms a film called a "bloom." Sugar may also rise to the surface in the same way. A gray or white haze that forms on top of the chocolate, "bloom" does not affect the quality or the taste of the chocolate in any way. If stored in a very humid place, chocolate will mold quickly. Always package chocolate tightly. Wrap it in foil and place it in a resealable plastic bag for the best protection. Chocolate and cocoa will absorb odors, and chocolate can become rancid because of poor storage. Cocoa becomes lumpy when allowed to absorb moisture.

Chapter 4

Baking Basics

Creating the Perfect Muffin

Here are just a few tips to help you produce consistently light and tender muffins.

1. Read the recipe in its entirety before you begin. Follow directions precisely; accuracy is critical in baking. Most failures come from using shortcuts.

2. Most ovens have hot spots. Always place the muffin pan in the middle of the center shelf. Muffins bake best and brown more evenly at this height. On the lowest shelf the bottoms brown too quickly, and on the highest shelf the tops brown too soon. (Note: These recipes are written for a standard gas or electric oven, not for a microwave oven.)

3. Always preheat the oven for at least 20 minutes. Muffins need a hot oven to rise and bake properly. Never place them into a cold oven. The result will be heavy, crumbly muffins. Preheat the oven 25 degrees higher than the actual baking temperature to compensate for the heat loss that occurs when you open the oven door. When muffins are ready for the oven, reduce the heat to the baking temperature. Recipes are written with their *baking* temperatures. Make

sure the oven temperature setting is correct when you put in the muffins.

4. Gather your equipment and ingredients to make sure you have everything at hand. As you are assembling the ingredients, prepare them as required—chopping, grating, or slicing—before you start making the batter.

5. Prepare muffin pans in advance. To prevent muffins from sticking, try a baking spray that contains flour. Baker's Joy works very well. You may also grease muffin cups with a very thin coating of solid shortening; do not use oil, butter, or margarine. Apply the shortening to the muffin pans, and then dust the cups with a thin coating of all-purpose flour. The cups should be thoroughly coated. Be sure to coat the inside surface as well as the top surface for muffins that rise above the pan. Paper or foil baking cups also work well, and eliminate the need for greasing the baking tins.

6. Always sift flour and dry ingredients together to blend, aerate, and lighten the flour. This will help prevent too compact of a texture. It is also important to distribute the baking soda and baking powder evenly. That helps you avoid muffins with yellowish holes and an acidic taste.

7. The best way to prepare muffins is by the two-bowl method. (*Note:* When in doubt, always mix ingredients in a bowl that is too large rather than too small.) That is, thoroughly combine the dry ingredients in one large mixing bowl, and the liquid ingredients in another mixing bowl.

Some recipes call for creaming the butter and sugar until light and fluffy before adding the remaining ingredients. To do this, make a well in the center of the dry ingredients. Add the liquid mixture all at once to the dry ingredients. Always pour the wet ingredients into the dry ingredients, not the other way around. Otherwise, you will have to stir too much. Fold the mixtures together just enough to incorporate the flour.

8. The single most important rule for successful muffins is, Do not overmix the final batter. This will overdevelop the gluten in the flour, producing flat, tough muffins with tunnels and peaked tops. At that point, your muffins have had it, and can be used as hockey pucks. Brief, light mixing ensures the tender, slightly

crumbly, even texture characteristic of a good muffin. The batter is best blended by hand using a large fork or wooden spoon. Allow any lumps that occur to remain; they will dissipate during baking. *Never* use an electric mixer or food processor for mixing. The machines tend to overbeat, producing a compacted muffin that rises less than it should.

9. It is important to keep the batter as cool as possible. This allows the baking soda or baking powder to begin action in the oven, where it's supposed to. If you can't bake the muffins at once, place the batter in the refrigerator until it can be used. Do not try to save the batter for longer than 4 to 6 hours.

10. Always start with a cool muffin pan. If you are using the same pan to continue baking, run cold water over the bottom of the tin to cool it. Dry and lightly grease the pan, then continue filling and baking.

11. Spoon the batter quickly into the prepared muffin pan. Fill any empty muffin wells with water to prevent scorching the tin. Place the muffins into the oven promptly. Batters with baking powder and baking soda need to be baked immediately (or kept cool), so the leavening power is not lost. You want the batter to start rising in the oven, not on the countertop. Note that while most recipes advise filling the muffin wells two-thirds full, I prefer to fill the cups generously to the brim, and even well above. This produces muffins with high rounded caps.

12. Baking times may vary depending on your oven, the altitude, and any substitutions you might have made. Do not open the oven door to check the muffins until they've been in for at least the minimum baking time. That is, if the range is 25 to 30 minutes, open the door only after 25 minutes. Keep in mind that each time the oven door is opened, the temperature drops 25 to 30 degrees. This will affect how well the muffins rise. Insert a cake tester or wooden pick into the center of the muffins to test for doneness. It should come out clean and moist, not wet. Do not overbake. The muffins will continue to bake in their own heat after you remove them from the oven to cool.

13. Allow muffins to stand a minute or two before removing them from the pan. They come out more easily that way. You

may have to help them out by running a knife along the side of each muffin cup and using the knife to support their weight. Place them on a wire cooling rack for a few minutes. The rack allows air to circulate around the muffins, keeping the bottoms and sides from steaming and becoming soggy.

14. Serve warm.

15. Store muffins that are not eaten immediately in a container that is loosely covered with a cloth. If you store muffins in a glass jar or cookie tin with a tightly fitting top, they will develop a moist, sticky coating. Also, don't leave a glass jar of muffins in a sunny window.

16. Store extra muffins in the freezer. It is the best way to save them because they freeze well. Allow the muffins to cool completely after baking. Wrap them in batches using heavy foil, or place them in airtight plastic containers or in gallon-size, reclosable freezer bags. Stored this way, muffins keep up to 3 months in the freezer. Use a self-adhesive tag to label each batch. Thaw muffins in aluminum foil at room temperature or heat at 300° to 350°F for about 15 to 20 minutes. You can also freeze baked muffins that have been individually wrapped and labeled. When reheating, place them in the oven in their foil wrappers.

17. To keep leftover muffins from drying out when reheating, cut them in half and sprinkle them lightly with fruit juice or water. Then place the muffins in a brown paper bag or wrap them lightly in foil, and warm them in a preheated 400°F oven for 10 to 15 minutes. You can warm them in a steamer as well. Another alternative is to wrap the muffin in a dry paper towel and heat it in the microwave on high for about 20 to 30 seconds.

With a little planning, just-baked muffins are easy to prepare in advance, and serve fresh, still warm from the oven, especially for breakfast. Prepare the dry and liquid ingredients in their separate bowls several hours or up to a day before baking. Refrigerate the liquid ingredients; do not add the melted butter until the last minute. Combine the two mixtures and bake in a preheated oven. Preparing fillings and streusels, and marinating dried fruits can be done ahead of time.

Making the Perfect Loaf

Quick breads are made in exactly the same way as muffins, except they are baked in loaf pans instead of muffin cups. Quick breads require a longer baking time—up to one hour at 350° to 375°F. Pan sizes vary, as do baking times. So remember to read the manufacturer's instructions.

1. Preheat the oven. Prepare the loaf pan by lightly but thoroughly greasing it with solid vegetable shortening. Add a small amount of all-purpose flour and dust the pan to leave a light, even coating on the shortening. Shake out any excess flour.

2. Prepare the batter and turn it into the pan. Lightly tap the pan on your work surface to eliminate any air pockets. Using a rubber spatula, smooth the batter. This is done so the loaf rises and browns evenly during baking. Place the loaf into the preheated oven.

3. Test for doneness by inserting a thin wooden skewer into the center of the loaf. It should come out clean and moist, but not wet. If the loaf isn't done, bake it a few minutes longer and then test it again. Expect to see a large, lengthwise crack in the thin, tender top crust. Remove the pan from the oven. Cool the loaf in the pan for 10 minutes, then unmold the loaf. Place the loaf, right side up, on a wire rack to cool. This keeps the crust firm and crisp. Allow the loaf to cool completely before slicing. Some loaves slice more easily after being wrapped and stored, at room temperature, for a day.

4. Using a sharp, thin-bladed knife, slice the loaf in a light, sawing motion. After cooling, the loaf can be wrapped tightly and kept at room temperature. Freeze it as you would muffins.

And finally, relax! Baking is a pleasure, not a chore. So take your time and enjoy what you're doing.

Chapter 5

Main-Course Muffins

With a character all their own, these mobile, hand-held minimeals are a departure from the usual muffin. Using these recipes as a guide, you can turn leftover vegetables, cheeses, and both cooked and smoked fish, meat, or poultry into scrumptious muffins. Made ahead for flexibility and convenience, and stocked in the freezer, these hearty muffins are an ideal way to avoid the temptation to grab fast foods. They are ready to reheat and eat! Satisfying richness and abundant protein combine to create savory muffins that are substantial enough to stand on their own.

Bacon Muffins

These are fabulous served with a hearty black-bean soup.

Yield: 10 large muffins   Preheat the oven to 450°F and prepare the pan.

In a medium bowl, blend well:
4 large eggs
2 cups sour cream
½ cup butter, melted and cooled

Add:
1 pound lean bacon (cooked, drained and crumbled)
½ cup chopped fresh chives

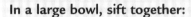

In a large bowl, sift together:
3½ cups all-purpose flour
2 tablespoons baking powder
½ teaspoon baking soda
1 tablespoon ground black pepper (optional)

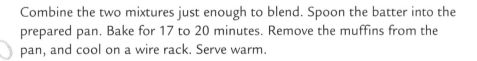

Combine the two mixtures just enough to blend. Spoon the batter into the prepared pan. Bake for 17 to 20 minutes. Remove the muffins from the pan, and cool on a wire rack. Serve warm.

Variations

Bacon Onion
Sauté 2 cups chopped onion, and add it to the wet ingredients.

Bacon-Onion Cornmeal
Prepare the Bacon Onion Muffins as directed, substituting 2 cups yellow cornmeal for 2 cups all-purpose flour.

Caraway Onion Muffins

These muffins are particularly good served with butter and Havarti cheese.

Yield: 12 large muffins   Preheat the oven to 400°F and prepare the pan.

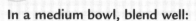

In a medium bowl, blend well:
4 large eggs
½ cup butter, melted and cooled
½ cup pure maple syrup or molasses
1½ cups buttermilk
1 tablespoon grated orange peel

Add:
2 cups minced onion
½ cup snipped fresh dill

In a large bowl, sift together:
2 cups rye flour
2 cups all-purpose flour
2 tablespoons baking powder
1 teaspoon baking soda

Add:
½ cup caraway seeds

Combine the two mixtures just enough to blend. Spoon the batter into the prepared pan. Bake for 18 to 20 minutes. Remove the muffins from the pan, and cool on a wire rack. Serve warm.

Variations

Nordic Ham and Rye
Add 2 cups diced Danish-style ham to the wet ingredients.

Ham and Cheddar
Add 1 cup diced ham and 1 cup grated sharp Cheddar cheese to the wet ingredients.

Chicken and Beef Tamale Muffins

These muffins need only soup and salad to make a soul-satisfying meal.

Yield: 12 to 14 large muffins

Preheat the oven to 425°F
and prepare the pan.

In a large bowl, blend well:
3 large eggs
½ cup butter, melted and cooled
1½ cups salsa or milk

Add:
½ lb. ground beef
　(browned and drained)
1 cup diced cooked chicken
1 cup grated Monterey Jack
　or Cheddar cheese
1 large onion, grated
1 (4.5-oz.) can chopped green
　chilies, drained
1 cup canned pinto beans, drained
1 (11-oz.) can whole-kernel corn,
　drained

In a large bowl, sift together:
3½ cups all-purpose flour
2 tablespoons baking powder

Add:
1 cup yellow cornmeal

 Combine the two mixtures just enough to blend. Spoon the batter into the prepared pan. Bake for 22 to 25 minutes. Remove the muffins from the pan, and cool on a wire rack. Serve warm.

Fig and Smoked Ham Muffins

This irresistible pairing of flavors creates a muffin that makes any meal memorable.

Yield: 12 large muffins   Preheat the oven to 400°F and prepare the pan.

In a medium bowl, blend well:
4 large eggs
2 cups buttermilk
½ cup butter, melted and cooled

Add:
2 cups diced smoked ham*

*Smithfield, Westphalian, or Black Forest are good choices for smoked ham.

In a large bowl, sift together:
3½ cups all-purpose flour
2 tablespoons baking powder
1 teaspoon baking soda
1 teaspoon cloves

Add:
1 cup cut-up dried figs
1 cup chopped toasted pecans

Combine the two mixtures just enough to blend. Spoon the batter into the prepared pan. Bake for 18 to 20 minutes. Remove the muffins from the pan, and cool on a wire rack. Serve warm.

Herb Muffins

These muffins exude the intoxicating scent of fresh herbs.

Yield: 12 large muffins

Preheat the oven to 400°F and prepare the pan.

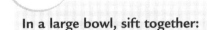

In a large bowl, blend well:
5 large eggs
½ cup butter, melted and cooled
1 cup plain yogurt

Add:
1 cup finely chopped scallions
2½ cups low-fat cottage cheese
1 cup minced fresh herbs,
   or 5 tablespoons dried

In a large bowl, sift together:
3½ cups all-purpose flour
1 tablespoon baking powder
1 tablespoon baking soda
1 tablespoon ground black pepper

Combine the two mixtures just enough to blend. Spoon the batter into the prepared pan. Bake for 20 to 25 minutes. Remove the muffins from the pan, and cool on a wire rack. Serve warm.

Suggested herbs for this recipe are: fresh dill, rosemary, basil, and thyme.

Pesto Muffins

Make these muffins with fresh basil if at all possible. They are a perfect complement to a variety of fish and shellfish.

Yield: 12 large muffins

Preheat the oven to 375°F and prepare the pan.

In a large bowl, blend well:
5 large eggs
½ cup butter, melted and cooled
1 cup honey

Add:
1 cup packed chopped fresh basil, or
    ¼ cup dried
4 cloves garlic, minced
2½ cups ricotta cheese
12 pitted Gaeta olives,* chopped
    (optional)

In a large bowl, sift together:
3½ cups all-purpose flour
4 teaspoons baking powder
1 tablespoon baking soda
1 tablespoon ground black pepper
1 cup grated Parmesan cheese

Add:
1 cup pine nuts or chopped walnuts

*Gaeta olives are available at Italian markets and specialty food stores. You may also use black olives.

Combine the two mixtures just enough to blend. Spoon the batter into the prepared pan. Bake for 20 to 25 minutes. Remove the muffins from the pan, and cool on a wire rack. Serve warm.

Pizza Muffins

These are savory, zesty muffins.

Yield: 12 large muffins

Preheat the oven to 425°F and prepare the pan.

In a large bowl, blend well:
2 large eggs
½ cup butter, melted and cooled
1 cup tomato sauce
1½ cups buttermilk

Add:
3 to 4 cups grated mozzarella
    or Fontina cheese
1 cup pepperoni or salami, sliced
    and quartered
1 (6-oz.) can pitted black olives,
    drained and quartered
1 cup chopped onion, sautéed
1 to 2 teaspoons crushed red pepper
    flakes
½ cup minced fresh parsley
1 tablespoon dried oregano

In a large bowl, sift together:
3½ cups all-purpose flour
½ cup freshly grated Parmesan
    or Romano cheese
¾ teaspoon baking soda
2 tablespoons baking powder

Combine the two mixtures just enough to blend. Spoon the batter into the prepared pan. Bake for 20 to 25 minutes. Remove the muffins from the pan, and cool on a wire rack. Serve warm.

Sausage Muffins

These muffins are delicious served with scrambled eggs.

Yield: 12 large muffins   Preheat the oven to 400°F and prepare the pan.

In a large bowl, blend well:
2 large eggs
½ cup butter, melted and cooled
2 cups milk

Add:
1 cup grated mozzarella
    or provolone cheese
1 cup *each* finely chopped red bell
    pepper and green onion
1 pound sausage (casings removed,
    browned, drained, and crumbled)

In a large bowl, sift together:
3½ cups all-purpose flour
2 tablespoons baking powder
½ teaspoon baking soda
1 tablespoon ground black pepper

Combine the two mixtures just enough to blend. Spoon the batter into the prepared pan. Bake for 20 to 25 minutes. Remove the muffins from the pan, and cool on a wire rack. Serve warm.

Variation

Cornmeal Sausage
Substitute 1½ cups yellow cornmeal for 1½ cups all-purpose flour.

Smoked Turkey and Wild Rice Muffins

The grain known as wild rice is, in fact, a cereal. Its special woodsy flavor complements smoked turkey beautifully.

Yield: 15 large muffins   Preheat the oven to 400°F and prepare the pan.

In a large bowl, blend well:
4 large eggs
½ cup butter, melted and cooled
2 cups milk

Add:
½ cup minced fresh parsley
2 cups cooked wild rice
1½ cups diced smoked turkey
    or chicken
1 cup grated apple
1 cup *each* finely chopped onion,
    celery, and mushroom
2 teaspoons dried sage

In a large bowl, sift together:
3½ cups all-purpose flour
2 tablespoons baking powder

Add:
1 cup golden raisins
1 cup chopped pecans

Combine the two mixtures just enough to blend. Spoon the batter into the prepared pan. Bake for 25 minutes. Remove the muffins from the pan, and cool on a wire rack. Serve warm.

Sour Cream—Chives Muffins

These muffins whip up high, handsome, and golden. They will rise very much like popovers.

Yield: 10 large muffins

Preheat the oven to 450°F and prepare the pan.

In a medium bowl, blend well:
5 large eggs
½ cup butter, melted and cooled
2 cups sour cream

Add:
1 cup chopped fresh chives or dill

In a large bowl, sift together:
3½ cups all-purpose flour
2 tablespoons baking soda
½ teaspoon baking powder

Combine the two mixtures just enough to blend. Spoon the batter into the prepared pan. Bake for 15 to 20 minutes. Remove the muffins from the pan, and transfer onto a wire rack. Serve hot or warm.

Southern Biscuit Muffins

These delicate muffins taste like angel biscuits. For a delicious shortcake dessert, split the warm muffins, fill them with juicy sugared berries (or any ripe juicy summer fruit) and cold freshly whipped cream. With dinner, they're made to soak up a rich gravy. Or serve them warm with butter and honey or jam for breakfast or brunch.

Yield: 12 large muffins   Preheat the oven to 400°F and prepare the pan.

In a large bowl, sift together:
5 cups all-purpose flour
½ cup sugar
3 tablespoons baking powder

Additional ingredients:
1½ cups butter, softened
2 cups cold milk

Cut the softened butter into the dry ingredients and blend until mixture resembles coarse crumbs. Then stir in the milk, blending just enough to moisten the flour mixture.

Spoon the batter into the prepared pan. Bake for 20 minutes. Remove the muffins from the pan, and cool on a wire rack. Serve warm.

Sun-Dried Tomato and Cheese Muffins

The bold flavors suggest that these muffins are not for the faint of heart! Sun-dried tomatoes have an intense flavor. The best ones are imported from Italy, and can be found in specialty and Italian food stores.

Yield: 12 large muffins

Preheat the oven to 400°F and prepare the pan.

In a large bowl, blend well:

5 large eggs

½ cup butter, melted and cooled

2 cups sour cream or plain yogurt

Add:

2 cups crumbled feta cheese

1½ cups oil-packed sun-dried
  tomatoes, drained and cut up

1 cup chopped, pitted Kalamata or
  other brine-cured black olives

4 large garlic cloves, minced

In a large bowl, sift together:

3 cups all-purpose flour

4 teaspoons baking powder

2 teaspoons baking soda

1 teaspoon dried basil

Combine the two mixtures just enough to blend. Spoon the batter into the prepared pan. Bake for 20 to 25 minutes. Remove the muffins from the pan, and cool on a wire rack. Serve warm.

Tex-Mex Muffins

These hot, spicy muffins are perfect for parties or picnics.

Yield: 12 large muffins   Preheat the oven to 400°F and prepare the pan.

In a large bowl, blend well:
2 large eggs
½ cup butter, melted and cooled
2 cups salsa or milk

Add:
1 cup grated Cheddar
  or Monterey Jack cheese
1 cup canned pinto beans, drained
1 cup finely chopped onion
1 cup chopped green chilies,
  or 1 to 2 (4.5-oz.) cans chopped
  green chilies, drained
1 lb. spicy sausage (casings
  removed, browned, drained,
  and crumbled)
½ cup chopped fresh cilantro
  or parsley
1 tablespoon minced fresh marjoram

In a large bowl, sift together:
3½ cups all-purpose flour
2 tablespoons baking powder
½ teaspoon baking soda
1 teaspoon ground cumin
1 tablespoon pure chili powder

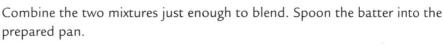

Combine the two mixtures just enough to blend. Spoon the batter into the prepared pan.

Bake for 20 to 25 minutes. Remove the muffins from the pan, and cool on a wire rack. Serve warm.

Tuna Muenster Melt Muffins

Enjoy tuna's versatility in a fabulous casserole muffin.

Yield: 12 large muffins   Preheat the oven to 425°F and prepare the pan.

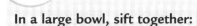

In a large bowl blend well:
4 large eggs
1 cup milk
1 cup low-fat cottage cheese
½ cup butter, melted and cooled

Add:
1 cup *each* chopped onion, celery,
   and red bell pepper
2 (6½-oz.) cans water-packed
   tuna, drained
2 cups grated Muenster cheese
¼ cup snipped fresh dill

In a large bowl, sift together:
3½ cups all-purpose flour
2 tablespoons baking powder
1 teaspoon baking soda
1 tablespoon ground black pepper

Add:
1 cup chopped walnuts

Combine the two mixtures just enough to blend. Spoon the batter into the prepared pan. Bake for 20 to 25 minutes. Remove the muffins from the pan, and cool on a wire rack. Serve warm.

Variation

Tuna Apple
Substitute 2 cups grated apple for the Muenster cheese.

Turkey and Swiss Cheese Muffins

These muffins are especially good for picnics.

Yield: 12 large muffins   Preheat the oven to 425°F and prepare the pan.

In a large bowl, blend well:
3 large eggs
½ cup butter, melted and cooled
2 cups buttermilk

Add:
2 cups diced cooked turkey
   or chicken
2 cups grated Swiss cheese
1 cup *each* finely chopped onion and
   celery
½ cup minced fresh parsley

In a large bowl, sift together:
3½ cups all-purpose flour
2 tablespoons baking powder
1 teaspoon baking soda
1 tablespoon ground black pepper

Combine the two mixtures just enough to blend. Spoon the batter into the prepared pan.

Bake for 20 minutes. Remove the muffins from the pan, and cool on a wire rack. Serve warm.

Variations

Chicken and Ham–Spinach
Substitute 1 cup *each* diced cooked chicken and ham for 2 cups turkey. Add 1 (10-oz.) package frozen chopped spinach, thawed and drained well, to the wet ingredients.

Ham and Blue Cheese
Substitute 2 cups diced cooked ham for the turkey, and 2 cups crumbled blue cheese for the Swiss cheese. Omit the onion and celery. Add 1 cup chopped pecans to the dry ingredients.

Chapter 6

Whole-Grain Muffins

Lingering over a leisurely morning meal is the ultimate indulgence! Forget about a fancy brunch; an honest, hearty breakfast is the most gratifying way to go. And what better way to begin the day than with these homey selections. Whole grains present a limitless source of low-cost, nutrition-rich eating pleasures. Coupled with fresh fruits, fruit and nut butters, omelets, cheeses, sausages, and bacon, or simply butter and pure maple syrup, these muffins complete a hearty meal indeed.

Remember when buying whole-grain flours, choose stone-ground flours whenever possible. Most stone-ground flours are milled by stone rollers propelled by water power. Since less heat is involved in the milling process, fewer nutrients are destroyed.

Apple Oatmeal Muffins

For a special breakfast or midmorning treat, these muffins are great served warm with peanut butter or apple butter.

Yield: 12 large muffins   Preheat the oven to 375°F and prepare the pan.

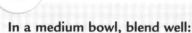

In a medium bowl, blend well:
2 large eggs
1 cup pure maple syrup
¾ cup milk
½ cup butter, melted and cooled
2 teaspoons vanilla extract

Add:
2 cups peeled, grated apples

In a large bowl, sift together:
3 cups all-purpose flour
2 tablespoons baking powder
½ teaspoon baking soda
¼ teaspoon cloves
1 tablespoon cinnamon
1 teaspoon nutmeg

Add:
3 cups rolled oats
1 cup raisins or currants

Combine the two mixtures just enough to blend. Spoon the batter into the prepared pan. Bake for 20 to 25 minutes. Remove the muffins from the pan, and cool on a wire rack. Serve warm.

Variations

Cranberry Apple
Add 2 cups fresh cranberries to the wet ingredients.

Coconut Oatmeal
Add 1 cup shredded coconut to the dry ingredients.

Apple Orange—Oat Bran Muffins

The honey and orange juice bring a delicious natural sweetness to these muffins.

Yield: 12 large muffins   Preheat the oven to 375°F and prepare the pan.

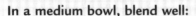

In a medium bowl, blend well:
3 large eggs
½ cup butter, melted and cooled
1 cup honey
1 cup fresh orange juice
1 tablespoon vanilla extract

Add:
1½ cups unsweetened applesauce
2 tablespoons grated orange peel
2 large apples, peeled and grated

In a large bowl, sift together:
2 cups all-purpose flour
1½ teaspoons baking soda
1 tablespoon baking powder
1 tablespoon cinnamon or nutmeg

Add:
2½ cups oat bran
1 cup raisins or cut-up dried apricots

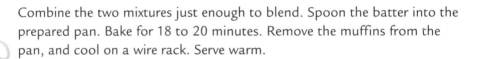

Combine the two mixtures just enough to blend. Spoon the batter into the prepared pan. Bake for 18 to 20 minutes. Remove the muffins from the pan, and cool on a wire rack. Serve warm.

Applesauce Bran Muffins

This is a hearty, fiber-rich muffin.

Yield: 12 large muffins   Preheat the oven to 400°F and prepare the pan.

In a large bowl, blend well:
2 large eggs
½ cup butter, melted and cooled
1 cup milk or fresh orange juice
1 cup packed brown sugar

Add:
2 cups unsweetened applesauce
3 cups 100% bran cereal (not flakes)

In a large bowl, sift together:
3 cups all-purpose flour
4 teaspoons baking powder
2 teaspoons baking soda
1 tablespoon cinnamon
1½ teaspoons nutmeg

Add:
1 cup raisins
1 cup cut-up dried apricots
1 cup chopped walnuts

Combine the two mixtures just enough to blend. Spoon the batter into the prepared pan. Bake for 20 to 25 minutes. Remove the muffins from the pan, and cool on a wire rack. Serve warm.

Variations

Pumpkin Bran
Substitute 2 cups mashed fresh or canned solid-pack pumpkin for the applesauce.

Grape-Nuts
Substitute 3 cups Grape-Nuts cereal for the bran cereal.

Banana Bran Muffins

These dark, rich, and sweet muffins will make your mouth water.

Yield: 12 large muffins   Preheat the oven to 375°F and prepare the pan.

In a medium bowl, blend well:
2 large eggs
½ cup butter, melted and cooled
½ cup honey or pure maple syrup
1 tablespoon vanilla extract
½ cup packed brown sugar

Add:
3 cups mashed very ripe bananas
2 tablespoons grated orange peel

In a large bowl, sift together:
2 cups all-purpose flour
½ cup whole-wheat flour
1 tablespoon baking powder
1½ teaspoons baking soda
1 tablespoon cinnamon
1 tablespoon nutmeg

Add:
1 cup miller's wheat bran or oat bran
1 cup chopped walnuts or pecans,
   or any cut-up dried fruit

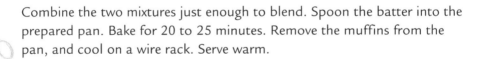

Combine the two mixtures just enough to blend. Spoon the batter into the prepared pan. Bake for 20 to 25 minutes. Remove the muffins from the pan, and cool on a wire rack. Serve warm.

Black Bean and Rice Muffins

These muffins are anything but common.

Yield: 12 large muffins

Preheat the oven to 400°F and prepare the pan.

In a large bowl, blend well:
2 large eggs
½ cup butter, melted and cooled
1 cup milk
1 cup low-fat cottage cheese

Add:
2 cups cooked rice
1 (15-oz.) can black beans, drained
½ cup minced fresh parsley
1 cup *each* finely chopped onion
   and red bell pepper

In a large bowl, sift together:
3½ cups all-purpose flour
2 tablespoons baking powder
½ teaspoon baking soda
½ teaspoon cayenne pepper

Combine the two mixtures just enough to blend. Spoon the batter into the prepared pan. Bake for 18 to 20 minutes. Remove the muffins from the pan, and cool on a wire rack. Serve warm.

Blue Cornmeal Muffins

Blue cornmeal, rare and wonderful, is a Native American food staple of the Southwest. The speckled blue corn, cultivated for centuries by the Pueblo Indians, has long been part of Native American tradition and religious ceremonies. Using piñon wood to smoke the corn and then grinding it with a lava wheel enhances its nutty taste. These muffins are a perfect complement to a hot bowl of chili, gazpacho, or other spicy Southwest dishes.

Yield: 14 large muffins   Preheat the oven to 450°F and prepare the pan.

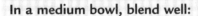

In a medium bowl, blend well:
4 large eggs

2 cups buttermilk or half-and-half

*Blue cornmeal is available in specialty food stores or can be purchased by mail order from the Pecos Valley Spice Company or M & S Produce. See Appendix 2.

In a large bowl, sift together:
2 cups all-purpose flour

⅔ cup sugar

2 tablespoons baking powder

2 teaspoons baking soda

4 cups blue cornmeal*

Cut in:
1¾ cups shortening or butter, softened Blend until mixture resembles coarse meal.

Combine the two mixtures just enough to blend. Spoon the batter into the prepared pan. Bake for 18 to 20 minutes. Remove the muffins from the pan, and cool on a wire rack. Serve warm.

Variations

Blue Cornmeal-Blueberry
After blending the batter, fold in 2 cups fresh blueberries.

Blue Corn and Ham
In a large skillet, heat 2 tablespoons vegetable oil. Sauté 2 cups chopped red bell pepper and 1 cup chopped onion until tender. Set vegetables aside to cool slightly. Add vegetables, ½ cup chopped fresh coriander, and 2 cups diced cooked ham to the wet ingredients.

Bonanza Muffins

Don't discard the whey when making yogurt cheese. Whey contains almost all the calcium and potassium found in milk products with none of the fat.

Yield: 13 large muffins   Preheat the oven to 375°F and prepare the pan.

In a medium bowl, blend well:
2 large eggs
½ cup butter, melted and cooled
1 cup honey
1 cup whey (or fresh orange juice)

Add:
1 cup grated carrots or apples
1 cup mashed very ripe bananas, or
   unsweetened applesauce

In a large bowl, sift together:
1½ cups all-purpose flour
¾ cup whole-wheat flour
¾ cup buckwheat flour
1 cup nonfat powdered milk
½ teaspoon baking soda
1 tablespoon baking powder

Add:
1½ cups miller's wheat or oat bran
1 cup wheat germ
1 cup cut-up dates, prunes, raisins,
   or dried apricots
½ cup toasted sunflower seeds
½ cup chopped walnuts
   or roasted unsalted peanuts

Combine the two mixtures just enough to blend. Spoon the batter into the prepared pan. Bake for 25 minutes. Remove the muffins from the pan, and cool on a wire rack. Serve warm.

Boston Brown Bread Muffins

These crusty muffins complement smoked meats and cheeses, hearty stews, and are a natural with baked beans. Serve them with plenty of fresh creamy butter.

Yield: 12 large muffins

Preheat the oven to 375°F and prepare the pan.

In a large bowl, blend well:
3 large eggs
½ cup butter, melted and cooled
½ cup molasses or honey
2 cups buttermilk

In a large bowl, sift together:
1 cup rye flour
1 cup whole-wheat flour
1 cup all-purpose flour
½ cup packed brown sugar
1 tablespoon baking soda

Add:
1 cup yellow cornmeal
1 cup dark raisins

Combine the two mixtures just enough to blend. Spoon the batter into the prepared pan. Bake for 20 to 25 minutes. Remove the muffins from the pan, and cool on a wire rack. Serve warm.

Variation

Fruited Brown Bread
In a medium bowl combine 1¾ cups (10-oz. package) cut-up pitted dates, 1¾ cups (10-oz. package) cut-up dried figs, and 1½ cups dark rum. Set aside to soak overnight. Drain and purée the fruit. Add puréed fruit to the wet ingredients. Omit the raisins.

Broccoli Cheddar Corn Muffins

These make delicious take-along munchies.

Yield: 14 large muffins   Preheat the oven to 450°F and prepare the pan.

In a large bowl, blend well:
3 large eggs
½ cup butter, melted and cooled
2½ cups buttermilk

Add:
1 cup finely chopped onion
2 (10-oz.) packages frozen chopped
   broccoli, thawed and drained well
2 cups grated extra-sharp Cheddar
   cheese

In a large bowl, sift together:
3 cups all-purpose flour
2 tablespoons baking soda
½ teaspoon baking powder
1 tablespoon ground black pepper

Add:
2 cups yellow cornmeal

Combine the two mixtures just enough to blend. Spoon the batter into the prepared pan. Bake for 18 minutes. Remove the muffins from the pan, and cool on a wire rack. Serve warm.

Buckwheat Muffins

These muffins with their fine texture and intriguing flavor are wonderful served with fresh creamy butter and warmed maple syrup.

Yield: 12 large muffins   Preheat the oven to 400°F and prepare the pan.

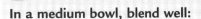

In a medium bowl, blend well:
2 large eggs
½ cup butter, melted and cooled
2 cups buttermilk
¼ cup honey

In a large bowl, sift together:
1½ cups all-purpose flour
2 cups buckwheat flour
1 tablespoon baking soda
1 cup packed light brown sugar
1 tablespoon baking powder
2 teaspoons cinnamon

Add:
1 cup currants

Combine the two mixtures just enough to blend. Spoon the batter into the prepared pan. Bake for 17 to 18 minutes. Remove the muffins from the pan, and cool on a wire rack. Serve warm.

Buttermilk Corn Muffins

This is a classic at its best.

Yield: 11 large muffins   Preheat the oven to 400°F and prepare the pan.

In a medium bowl, blend well:
2 large eggs
½ cup butter, melted and cooled
2 cups buttermilk

In a large bowl, sift together:
2 cups all-purpose flour
⅔ to ¾ cup sugar
1 tablespoon baking powder
1 tablespoon baking soda

Add:
2¼ cups yellow cornmeal

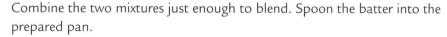

Combine the two mixtures just enough to blend. Spoon the batter into the prepared pan.

Bake for 18 to 20 minutes. Remove the muffins from the pan, and cool on a wire rack. Serve warm.

Variations

Cornmeal–Oat Bran
Substitute 1 cup oat bran for 1 cup cornmeal.

Cornmeal–Wheat Germ
Substitute 1 cup wheat germ for 1 cup cornmeal.

More variations of . . . Buttermilk Corn Muffins

Honey-Grain Cornmeal
Substitute 1 cup honey for 1 cup buttermilk. Omit the sugar. Substitute ½ cup *each* oat bran, rolled oats, and wheat germ for 1½ cups cornmeal.

Maple-Pecan Corn
Substitute 1 cup pure maple syrup for 1 cup buttermilk. Omit the sugar.
Add 1 cup chopped toasted pecans to the dry ingredients. Add 1 bottle (3-oz.) 100 percent real bacon bits to the wet ingredients (optional).

Carrot Corn
Add 2 cups grated carrots to the wet ingredients.

Bourbon Corn
Substitute ½ cup bourbon whiskey for ½ cup buttermilk.

Jalapeño Corn
Spoon half the batter into the pan. Top with 1 teaspoon *each* softened cream cheese and jalapeño jelly, then cover with the remaining batter. Bake as directed.

Sugar is optional in the following recipes.

Swiss Cornmeal
Add 2 cups grated Swiss cheese to the wet ingredients.

Ham Cornmeal
Add 2 cups diced ham to the wet ingredients.

Chives and Black Pepper–Cornmeal
Substitute 1 cup sour cream for 1 cup buttermilk. Add 1 cup chopped fresh chives to the wet ingredients. Add 2 tablespoons coarsely ground black pepper to the dry ingredients.

Cornmeal Herb
Add ¼ cup *each* chopped fresh parsley, basil, and dill; 1 teaspoon *each* dried oregano and sage; and ½ teaspoon *each* dried marjoram and thyme to the wet ingredients.

Bacon Cornmeal
Add 1 pound lean bacon (cooked, drained, and crumbled) to the wet ingredients.

Even more variations of . . . Buttermilk Corn Muffins

Cheddar Cornmeal
Add to the wet ingredients, 2 cups grated sharp Cheddar cheese,
1 (17-oz.) can cream-style corn, and 1 large onion, grated.

Chili and Cheese–Cornmeal
Add to the wet ingredients, 1 cup *each* grated Cheddar and Monterey Jack cheese, and 1
(4.5-oz.) can chopped green chilies, drained.

Blue Cheese–Cornmeal
Add 2 to 3 cups crumbled blue cheese, and 1 cup finely chopped scallions to the wet ingredients. Add 1 tablespoon ground black pepper to the dry ingredients.

Spinach and Cheese–Cornmeal
Add 1 (10-oz.) package frozen chopped spinach (thawed and drained well) and 2 cups
grated sharp Cheddar cheese to the wet ingredients. Add 1 teaspoon cayenne pepper to
the dry ingredients.

Buttermilk Oatmeal Muffins

This superb, crusty muffin is perfect with your favorite jams and fruit preserves.

Yield: 12 large muffins   Preheat the oven to 400°F and prepare the pan.

In a medium bowl, blend well:
2 large eggs
1 cup buttermilk
½ cup butter, melted and cooled
1 tablespoon vanilla extract
1½ cups pure maple syrup

In a large bowl, sift together:
2 cups all-purpose flour
1 cup packed brown sugar
2 tablespoons baking powder
1 teaspoon baking soda
1 tablespoon cinnamon

Add:
3 cups rolled oats

Combine the two mixtures just enough to blend. Spoon the batter into the prepared pan. Bake for 18 to 20 minutes. Remove the muffins from the pan, and cool on a wire rack. Serve warm.

Variations

Oatmeal Blueberry
After blending the batter, fold in 2 cups fresh blueberries (or blackberries).

Oatmeal Cranberry
Add 1 cup chopped walnuts to the dry ingredients. After blending the batter, fold in 2 cups fresh cranberries.

More variations of . . . Buttermilk Oatmeal Muffins

Oatmeal Raisin
Add to the dry ingredients ¾ cup *each* raisins, chopped walnuts, and shredded coconut.

Oatmeal Fig
Add to the dry ingredients 1 cup cut-up dried figs and 1 cup chopped pecans.

Chocolate Chip–Oatmeal
Add to the dry ingredients 1 cup mini chocolate chips and ½ cup chopped walnuts.

Peanut Butter–Oatmeal
For this variation use the ½ cup butter softened. Cream together the butter and 1½ cups smooth peanut butter. Blend in eggs, buttermilk, vanilla, and maple syrup. Add 1 cup raisins, mini–chocolate chips, or chopped unsalted peanuts to the dry ingredients.

Orange Oatmeal
Substitute 1 cup fresh orange juice for the buttermilk and add 2 tablespoons grated orange peel to the wet ingredients.

Cherry Oatmeal
Substitute 1 cup fresh orange juice for the buttermilk and add 2 tablespoons grated orange peel to the wet ingredients. Add 1 (18 ounce) can pitted sour cherries, drained and cut up, to the dry ingredients.

Buttery Corn Muffins

This corn muffin has a velvety texture.

Yield: 9 large muffins

Preheat the oven to 425°F and prepare the pan.

In a medium bowl, blend well:
3 large eggs
2 cups buttermilk or half-and-half

In a large bowl, sift together:
2 cups all-purpose flour
2 tablespoons baking powder
1 teaspoon baking soda
¾ cup sugar

Cut in:
1 cup butter, softened. Blend until the mixture resembles coarse meal.

Add:
2 cups yellow cornmeal

Combine the two mixtures just enough to blend. Spoon the batter into the prepared pan. Bake for 18 to 20 minutes. Remove the muffins from the pan, and cool on a wire rack. Serve warm.

Caraway Rye Muffins

Serve these muffins with hot pastrami, ham, or smoked cheeses.

Yield: 12 large muffins   Preheat the oven to 425°F and prepare the pan.

In a medium bowl, blend well:
3 large eggs
½ cup butter, melted and cooled
2 cups buttermilk
¼ cup carob powder

In a large bowl, sift together:
1½ cups all-purpose flour
2 cups rye flour
2 tablespoons baking powder
1 teaspoon baking soda
¾ cup packed brown sugar

Add:
½ cup caraway seeds

Combine the two mixtures just enough to blend. Spoon the batter into the prepared pan. Bake for 15 to 20 minutes. Remove the muffins from the pan, and cool on a wire rack. Serve warm.

Cornbread Muffins

A savory muffin you can serve alongside chili, or with honey and butter for breakfast.

Yield: 12 large muffins   Preheat the oven to 500°F and prepare the pan.

In a large bowl, blend well:
3 large eggs
½ cup butter, melted and cooled
3 cups buttermilk, milk,
  or half-and-half

In a large bowl, sift together:
1 cup all-purpose flour
2 tablespoons sugar
2 tablespoons baking powder
1 teaspoon baking soda

Add:
3 cups yellow cornmeal

Combine the two mixtures just enough to blend. Spoon the batter into the prepared pan. Bake for 15 minutes. Remove the muffins from the pan, and cool on a wire rack. Serve warm.

Variation

Cheese and Turkey–Cornbread
Add 1½ cups *each* grated Cheddar cheese and diced cooked smoked turkey to the wet ingredients.

Granola Muffins

A wonderfully satisfying muffin that has a crispy golden crust.

Yield: 12 large muffins

Preheat the oven to 400°F and prepare the pan.

In a medium bowl, blend well:
4 large eggs
½ cup butter, melted and cooled
2 cups buttermilk
2 teaspoons vanilla or maple extract

In a large bowl, sift together:
3 cups all-purpose flour
¾ cup packed brown sugar
2 tablespoons baking powder
1 teaspoon baking soda
1 tablespoon cinnamon

Add:
4 cups granola cereal

Combine the two mixtures just enough to blend. Spoon the batter into the prepared pan. Bake for 18 to 20 minutes. Remove the muffins from the pan, and cool on a wire rack. Serve warm.

Variation

Applesauce Granola
Substitute 2 cups unsweetened applesauce for the buttermilk.

Granola Carrot Muffins

Filled with carrots, walnuts, and raisins, these muffins are delicious spread with ricotta sweetened with a little honey.

Yield: 12 large muffins   Preheat the oven to 400°F and prepare the pan.

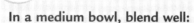

In a medium bowl, blend well:
2 large eggs
½ cup butter, melted and cooled
1 tablespoon vanilla extract
2 cups buttermilk

Add:
2 cups grated carrots or peeled,
   grated raw sweet potato

In a large bowl, sift together:
3 cups all-purpose flour
1 cup packed brown sugar
1 teaspoon baking soda
2 tablespoons baking powder
1 tablespoon cinnamon
1 teaspoon mace or nutmeg

Add:
4 cups granola cereal
1 cup chopped walnuts
½ cup raisins

Combine the two mixtures just enough to blend. Spoon the batter into the prepared pan. Bake for 20 minutes. Remove the muffins from the pan, and cool on a wire rack. Serve warm.

Honey and Fig Whole-Wheat Muffins

Stuffed with figs, nuts, and wheat germ, these muffins make a marvelous morning meal.

Yield: 12 large muffins   Preheat the oven to 375°F and prepare the pan.

In a medium bowl, blend well:
2 large eggs
½ cup butter, melted and cooled
1 cup honey
1 cup milk

In a large bowl, sift together:
2 cups whole-wheat flour
1 cup all-purpose flour
1 cup wheat germ
4 teaspoons baking powder
1 tablespoon cinnamon
1 tablespoon nutmeg

Add:
2 cups cut-up dried figs
1 cup chopped walnuts

Combine the two mixtures just enough to blend. Spoon the batter into the prepared pan. Bake for 25 to 30 minutes. Remove the muffins from the pan, and cool on a wire rack. Serve warm.

Variation

Fig and Date
Substitute 1 cup cut-up pitted dates for 1 cup figs.

Honey Bran Muffins

The natural goodness of bran and apples is sweetened with golden honey and scented with spice.

Yield: 12 large muffins   Preheat the oven to 375°F and prepare the pan.

In a medium bowl, blend well:
2 large eggs
1 cup honey
1 cup butter, melted and cooled
¾ cup milk
¼ cup vegetable oil

Add:
2 large apples, peeled and grated

In a large bowl, sift together:
1½ cups whole-wheat flour
1½ cups all-purpose flour
½ teaspoon baking soda
1 tablespoon baking powder
1 tablespoon cinnamon

Add:
3 cups miller's wheat bran
1 cup raisins or cut-up pitted dates

Combine the two mixtures just enough to blend. Spoon the batter into the prepared pan. Bake for 25 to 30 minutes. Remove the muffins from the pan, and cool on a wire rack. Serve warm.

Variation

Pecan–Honey Bran
Add to the dry ingredients, ½ teaspoon *each* ginger and nutmeg.
Substitute 1 cup chopped pecans or walnuts for the raisins or dates.

Honey-Glazed Bran Muffins

This is a delicious muffin with a superb glaze.

Yield: 12 to 14 large muffins

Preheat the oven to 375°F.

In a large bowl, blend well:
3 large eggs
½ cup butter, melted and cooled
½ cup honey
2 cups buttermilk
1 teaspoon vanilla extract

Add:
3½ cups (two 10-oz. packages)
    pitted dates, puréed
1 cup miller's wheat bran or rolled
    oats

In a large bowl, sift together:
3 cups all-purpose flour
1 tablespoon baking soda
2 teaspoons nutmeg

Glaze:
¼ cup butter, softened
¼ cup granulated sugar
¼ cup brown sugar, firmly packed
⅓ cup honey
2 tablespoons boiling water

In a medium bowl, cream the butter, sugar, and brown sugar, until the mixture is light and fluffy. Beat in the honey and boiling water. Then, using a pastry brush, coat the bottom and sides of the muffin cups generously with the glaze. Reserve any remaining glaze.

Combine the two mixtures just enough to blend. Spoon the batter into the prepared pan.

Bake for 20 to 25 minutes.

Brush the tops of the muffins with the reserved glaze while they are still hot from the oven. Remove the muffins from the pan, and cool on a wire rack. Serve warm.

Maple Pecan–Rice Bran Muffins

Earthy and wonderful, these muffins are delicious with butter and homemade jam.

Yield: 12 large muffins   Preheat the oven to 350°F and prepare the pan.

In a medium bowl, blend well:
2 large eggs
½ cup butter, melted and cooled
1 cup milk
1 cup pure maple syrup

In a large bowl, sift together:
2 cups all-purpose flour
½ cup packed light brown sugar
  (optional)
2 tablespoons baking powder

Add:
1½ cups rice bran (not rice bran
cereal)
½ cup yellow cornmeal
1 cup chopped pecans

Combine the two mixtures just enough to blend. Spoon the batter into the prepared pan. Bake for 25 minutes. Remove the muffins from the pan, and cool on a wire rack. Serve warm.

Oat Bran Muffins

With the natural sweetness and mild, nutty taste of oat bran, these muffins are delicious warm. Just spread with applesauce, ricotta cheese, or a bit of sweet butter.

Yield: 12 large muffins   Preheat the oven to 375°F and prepare the pan.

In a medium bowl, blend well:
3 large eggs
½ cup butter, melted and cooled
1 cup honey
1 cup plain yogurt
2 teaspoons vanilla extract

Add:
1½ cups unsweetened applesauce
1 tablespoon grated orange peel

In a large bowl, sift together:
2 cups all-purpose flour
½ teaspoon baking soda
1 tablespoon baking powder
1 tablespoon cinnamon

Add:
2½ cups oat bran

Combine the two mixtures just enough to blend. Spoon the batter into the prepared pan. Bake for 18 to 20 minutes. Remove the muffins from the pan, and cool on a wire rack. Serve warm.

Variations

Chocolate–Oat Bran
Add ½ cup unsweetened cocoa powder to the wet ingredients, and ½ cup poppy seeds to the dry ingredients.

Maple Raisin–Oat Bran
Substitute 1 cup pure maple syrup for the honey, and 1½ cups mashed very ripe banana for the applesauce. Add 1 cup raisins and ¾ cup chopped pecans to the dry ingredients.

More variations of . . . Oat Bran Muffins

Orange Bran
Substitute 1 cup fresh orange juice for the yogurt.

Cherry Apricot–Oat Bran
Add ¾ cup *each* cut-up dried cherries and dried apricots, and 1 cup chopped almonds or walnuts to the dry ingredients.

Banana-Oat Bran
Fold in 2 cups cut-up banana, after the batter has been blended. Add 1 cup chopped pecans or walnuts to the dry ingredients.

Maple Nut-Oat Bran
Substitute 1 cup pure maple syrup for the honey, and 1 cup rolled oats for 1 cup oat bran. Add ½ cup *each* chopped pecans and almonds to the dry ingredients.

Pancake Muffins

A delicious new take on a breakfast favorite, serve these muffins with crisp bacon and eggs.

Yield: 12 large muffins   Preheat the oven to 425°F and prepare the pan.

In a medium bowl, blend well:
5 large eggs
1 cup plain yogurt or buttermilk
2 teaspoons maple or vanilla extract
1 cup pancake syrup
  (not pure maple syrup)

In a large bowl, sift together:
3½ cups pancake mix
1 tablespoon cinnamon
¾ cup packed brown sugar

Add:
3 cups rolled oats
1 cup chopped walnuts (optional)

Combine the two mixtures just enough to blend. Spoon the batter into the prepared pan. Bake for 15 to 20 minutes. Remove the muffins from the pan, and cool on a wire rack. Serve warm.

Peanut Banana–Bran Muffins

Kids love these muffins for an afterschool treat. Just split them open and spread with chunky peanut butter.

Yield: 12 large muffins   Preheat the oven to 375°F and prepare the pan.

In a large bowl, blend well:
2 large eggs
½ cup butter, melted and cooled
½ cup honey
1 cup buttermilk
2 teaspoons vanilla extract

Add:
2 cups mashed very ripe bananas

In a large bowl, sift together:
1½ cups whole-wheat flour
1½ cups all-purpose flour
1 tablespoon baking soda
½ cup sugar

Add:
1½ cups miller's wheat bran
1 cup chopped unsalted roasted
    peanuts, raisins, or pitted dates

Combine the two mixtures just enough to blend. Spoon the batter into the prepared pan. Bake for 20 to 25 minutes. Remove the muffins from the pan, and cool on a wire rack. Serve warm.

Pineapple Corn Muffins

These muffins are wonderful served with a tangy cranberry and orange relish at holiday meals or with fried ham and eggs for brunch.

Yield: 12 large muffins   Preheat the oven to 425°F and prepare the pan.

In a large bowl, blend well:
5 large eggs
½ cup butter, melted and cooled
½ cup milk
1 tablespoon vanilla extract
2 tablespoons grated orange peel

Add:
2 cups low-fat cottage
   or ricotta cheese
1 (8-oz.) can crushed pineapple
   in juice, undrained.

In a large bowl, sift together:
3½ cups all-purpose flour
1 cup sugar
4 teaspoons baking powder
4 teaspoons baking soda
1 tablespoon cinnamon

Add:
2 cups yellow cornmeal
1 cup chopped pecans

Combine the two mixtures just enough to blend. Spoon the batter into the prepared pan. Bake for 20 to 22 minutes. Remove the muffins from the pan, and cool on a wire rack. Serve warm.

Variations

Blueberry Corn
After blending the batter, fold in 2 cups fresh blueberries or huckleberries.

Apricot Corn
Add 1 cup cut-up dried apricots to the dry ingredients.

Cranberry Cornmeal
Add ½ cup raisins to the dry ingredients. After blending the batter, fold in 2 cups fresh cranberries.

Pinto Bean Muffins

Whether packing lunches for children or adults, try these for a delicious change of pace.

Yield: 12 large muffins   Preheat the oven to 375°F and prepare the pan.

In a medium bowl, blend well:
4 large eggs
½ cup butter, melted and cooled
1 cup honey
1 cup milk
1 tablespoon vanilla extract

Add:
2 cups mashed pinto beans,
  cooked or canned

In a large bowl, sift together:
3 cups all-purpose flour
1 tablespoon baking powder
1 tablespoon baking soda
1½ teaspoons *each* cinnamon
  and nutmeg

Add:
1 cup yellow cornmeal
1 cup raisins

Combine the two mixtures just enough to blend. Spoon the batter into the prepared pan. Bake for 18 to 20 minutes. Remove the muffins from the pan, and cool on a wire rack. Serve warm.

Pumpernickel Currant Muffins

Serve this hearty muffin with stews or thick soups, robust meats and mustards, thick wedges of sharp Cheddar, or cream cheese and marmalade.

Yield: 12 large muffins   Preheat the oven to 400°F and prepare the pan.

In a medium bowl, blend well:
3 large eggs
½ cup butter, melted and cooled
½ cup molasses
⅓ cup unsweetened cocoa powder
1 (12-oz.) can lager beer,
    at room temperature
1 tablespoon grated orange peel

In a large bowl, sift together:
1½ cups all-purpose flour
2 cups rye flour
2 tablespoons baking soda
1 tablespoon allspice
½ cup packed brown sugar

Add:
1 cup yellow cornmeal
¼ cup caraway seeds
1 cup currants

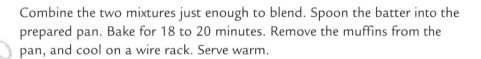

Combine the two mixtures just enough to blend. Spoon the batter into the prepared pan. Bake for 18 to 20 minutes. Remove the muffins from the pan, and cool on a wire rack. Serve warm.

Rice Muffins

Here's a delicious way to make the most of leftover rice.

Yield: 12 large muffins 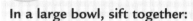 Preheat the oven to 375°F and prepare the pan.

In a large bowl, blend well:

4 large eggs

⅔ cup honey or pure maple syrup

½ cup butter, melted and cooled

⅔ cup milk

1 teaspoon vanilla or almond extract

Add:

2 cups cooked white or brown rice

2 tablespoons grated orange peel

In a large bowl, sift together:

2½ cups all-purpose flour

2 tablespoons baking powder

1 tablespoon cinnamon

½ teaspoon nutmeg

Add:

1 cup currants, raisins,
   or cut-up dried apricots

 Combine the two mixtures just enough to blend. Spoon the batter into the prepared pan. Bake for 20 to 25 minutes. Remove the muffins from the pan, and cool on a wire rack. Serve warm.

Sour Cream—Bran Muffins

Warm from the oven, these muffins make a luxurious start to any morning.

Yield: 12 large muffins   Preheat the oven to 400°F and prepare the pan.

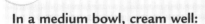

In a medium bowl, cream well:
½ cup packed brown sugar
½ cup butter, softened

Blend in:
2 large eggs
2 cups sour cream
½ cup molasses

In a large bowl, sift together:
2 cups all-purpose flour
1 tablespoon cinnamon
1 tablespoon baking soda

Add:
2 cups miller's wheat bran
1 cup raisins (optional)

Combine the two mixtures just enough to blend. Spoon the batter into the prepared pan. Bake for 18 to 20 minutes. Remove the muffins from the pan, and cool on a wire rack. Serve warm.

Variation

Cheddar Bran
Omit the raisins. Add 1 cup grated sharp Cheddar cheese to the wet ingredients.

Tex-Mex Pumpkin Corn Muffins

A perfect choice for chili, red beans and rice, or a tangy Spanish omelet.

Yield: 12 large muffins   Preheat the oven to 375°F and prepare the pan.

In a medium bowl, blend well:
2 large eggs
½ cup butter, melted and cooled
2 cups buttermilk or nonfat plain
  yogurt
1 cup mashed fresh or canned
  solid-pack pumpkin

Add:
2 (4.5-oz.) cans chopped green
  chilies, drained
2 cups grated Cheddar cheese

In a large bowl, sift together:
2 cups all-purpose flour
¼ cup sugar
1 tablespoon baking powder
1 tablespoon baking soda
1 teaspoon chili powder

Add:
2¼ cups yellow cornmeal

Combine the two mixtures just enough to blend. Spoon the batter into the prepared pan. Bake for 20 minutes. Remove the muffins from the pan, and cool on a wire rack. Serve warm.

Variation

Spicy Yam
Omit the green chilies and Cheddar cheese. Substitute 1 cup cold strong coffee for 1 cup buttermilk, 1 cup mashed yams or sweet potatoes for the pumpkin, and 1 tablespoon cinnamon for the 1 teaspoon chili powder. Add 1 teaspoon Tabasco sauce to the wet ingredients.

Whole-Wheat Molasses Bran Muffins

Delicious with fruit butters, these muffins are equally appealing with assorted sliced cheeses.

Yield: 12 large muffins

Preheat the oven to 375°F and prepare the pan.

In a medium bowl, blend well:
2 large eggs
1½ cups molasses
½ cup butter, melted and cooled
2 cups buttermilk or plain yogurt

In a large bowl, sift together:
2¾ cups whole-wheat flour
3½ teaspoons baking soda
1 tablespoon cinnamon

Add:
3 cups miller's wheat bran
1 cup raisins
1 tablespoon anise seed

Combine the two mixtures just enough to blend. Spoon the batter into the prepared pan. Bake for 25 minutes. Remove the muffins from the pan, and cool on a wire rack. Serve warm.

Variation

Chocolate Chip–Bran
Add 1 cup mini–chocolate chips to the dry ingredients. Substitute 1 cup cut-up dried apricots for the raisins.

Chapter 7

Fruit and Vegetable Muffins

With a wealth of fruits and vegetables to inspire you once you've sampled some of these recipes, plain muffins will hardly seem the same. In addition to their marvelous flavor and texture, fruits and vegetables provide many health benefits like high complex carbohydrates, high fiber, high mineral and vitamin content, a low fat content, and few calories. These moist, tender muffins, bursting with juicy prizes from the garden, fit menus that span from breakfast to dinner.

Apple Butter Muffins

A pocket of apple butter is nestled inside each muffin for a bit of unexpected flavor.

Yield: 12 large muffins   Preheat the oven to 400°F and prepare the pan.

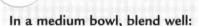

In a medium bowl, blend well:
2 large eggs
½ cup butter, melted and cooled
1½ cups milk

Filling:
Pure apple butter

In a large bowl, sift together:
3 cups all-purpose flour
⅔ cup sugar
4 teaspoons baking powder
1 teaspoon cinnamon
1 teaspoon nutmeg
½ teaspoon allspice
¼ teaspoon ginger

Add:
1 cup chopped pecans

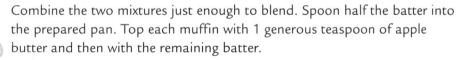

Combine the two mixtures just enough to blend. Spoon half the batter into the prepared pan. Top each muffin with 1 generous teaspoon of apple butter and then with the remaining batter.

In a small bowl, mix ½ cup granulated sugar, 4 teaspoons cinnamon, and ½ teaspoon nutmeg. Sprinkle the tops generously with this Cinnamon Sugar, keeping any leftover for another use.

Bake for 20 minutes. Remove the muffins from the pan, and cool on a wire rack. Serve warm.

Apple Carrot Muffins

Brimming with sweet apples and carrots, fragrant spices, and crunchy walnuts, these muffins are perfect for a special brunch or a midmorning coffee break.

Yield: 12 large muffins   Preheat the oven to 400°F and prepare the pan.

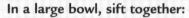

In a large bowl, blend well:
4 large eggs
1 cup sour cream
½ cup butter, melted and cooled
1 tablespoon vanilla extract

Add:
1¾ cups peeled, grated apples
1¾ cups grated carrots

In a large bowl, sift together:
3 cups all-purpose flour
2 tablespoons baking soda
1 cup sugar
1 teaspoon cinnamon
1 teaspoon *each* allspice and
    nutmeg

Add:
2 cups chopped walnuts or pecans

Combine the two mixtures just enough to blend. Spoon the batter into the prepared pan.

In a small bowl, mix ½ cup granulated sugar, 4 teaspoons cinnamon, and ½ teaspoon nutmeg. Sprinkle the tops generously with this Cinnamon Sugar, keeping any leftover for another use.

Bake for 20 to 22 minutes. Remove the muffins from the pan, and cool on a wire rack. Serve warm.

Apple Cinnamon Muffins

These plump little bundles are loaded with fruit, nuts, and topped off with the sweet scent of cinnamon sugar.

Yield: 12 large muffins   Preheat the oven to 400°F and prepare the pan.

In a medium bowl, blend well:
3 large eggs
½ cup butter, melted and cooled
1 cup sour cream or plain yogurt
1 tablespoon vanilla extract

Add:
3 cups peeled, grated apples

In a large bowl, sift together:
1½ cups whole-wheat flour
1½ cups all-purpose flour
2 tablespoons baking powder
1 cup packed brown sugar
1 tablespoon cinnamon
¼ teaspoon *each* allspice and nutmeg

Add:
1 cup chopped walnuts
1 cup raisins

Combine the two mixtures just enough to blend. Spoon the batter into the prepared pan.

In a small bowl, mix ½ cup granulated sugar, 4 teaspoons cinnamon, and ½ teaspoon nutmeg. Sprinkle the tops generously with this Cinnamon Sugar, keeping any leftover for another use.

Bake for 20 minutes. Remove the muffins from the pan, and cool on a wire rack. Serve warm.

Variation

Apple Ginger
Add ½ cup peeled, grated fresh ginger to the wet ingredients.

Apple Honey Muffins

These muffins are earthy and robust.

Yield: 12 large muffins   Preheat the oven to 375°F and prepare the pan.

In a medium bowl, blend well:
2 large eggs
1 cup honey
¾ cup apple juice
½ cup butter, melted and cooled

Add:
2 cups peeled, grated apples
¾ cup unsweetened applesauce

In a large bowl, sift together:
2 cups all-purpose flour
1 cup whole-wheat flour
½ teaspoon baking soda
1 tablespoon baking powder
1 tablespoon nutmeg or cinnamon

Add:
2 cups wheat germ
2 cups chopped walnuts or pecans
1 cup raisins

Combine the two mixtures just enough to blend. Spoon the batter into the prepared pan. Bake for 25 to 30 minutes. Remove the muffins from the pan, and cool on a wire rack. Serve warm.

Applesauce Spice Muffins

These are great to pack in an autumn picnic basket with a Thermos of hot apple cider or mulled wine.

Yield: 12 large muffins   Preheat the oven to 425°F and prepare the pan.

In a medium bowl, blend well:
4 large eggs
½ cup butter, melted and cooled
1 tablespoon vanilla extract
¼ cup unsweetened cocoa powder

Add:
2 cups unsweetened applesauce
¼ cup apple brandy

In a large bowl, sift together:
3½ cups all-purpose flour
½ teaspoon baking soda
2 tablespoons baking powder
1 cup packed brown sugar
2 teaspoons cinnamon
½ teaspoon *each* allspice, cloves,
   and nutmeg

Add:
1 cup raisins or currants
1 cup chopped walnuts or pecans

Combine the two mixtures just enough to blend. Spoon the batter into the prepared pan. Bake for 20 minutes. Remove the muffins from the pan, and cool on a wire rack. Serve warm.

Variations

Applesauce–Chocolate Chip
Substitute 1 cup mini–chocolate chips for the raisins or nuts.

Whole-Wheat Applesauce
Substitute 2 cups whole-wheat flour for 2 cups all-purpose flour. One cup cut-up pitted dates may be substituted for raisins.

Applesauce Cheddar
Add 1½ cups grated sharp Cheddar cheese to the wet ingredients.

Apricot Applesauce
Add 1 cup cut-up dried apricots to the dry ingredients.

Apricot Muffins

Sweet-tart apricots, a hint of orange, and toasted almonds create a sumptuous muffin.

Yield: 12 large muffins   Preheat the oven to 400°F and prepare the pan.

In a medium bowl, blend well:
1½ cups packed brown sugar
½ cup butter, melted and cooled
3 large eggs
2 cups sour cream
1 tablespoon vanilla extract
2 tablespoons grated orange peel

In a large bowl, sift together:
3 cups all-purpose flour
2 teaspoons baking soda
4 teaspoons baking powder
1 tablespoon cardamom
1 teaspoon nutmeg

Add:
2 cups cut-up dried apricots
1 cup slivered almonds, toasted
1 cup shredded coconut

Combine the two mixtures just enough to blend. Spoon the batter into the prepared pan. Bake for 25 minutes. Remove the muffins from the pan, and cool on a wire rack. Serve warm.

Variations

Apricot Amaretto
Pour 1 tablespoon Amaretto liqueur over each muffin while they are still hot from the oven and before you remove them from the pan. Allow the Amaretto to soak through, and then transfer them to a wire rack. Serve warm.

Apricot Date
Substitute 1 cup cut-up pitted dates for 1 cup apricots.

Apricot Cherry
Omit 1 cup apricots and add 1 (18-oz.) can pitted sour cherries, drained and halved, to the dry ingredients.

Apricot Blueberry Muffins

For a sweet, tangy dessert, dust these muffins with a bit of powdered sugar.

Yield: 12 large muffins   Preheat the oven to 400°F and prepare the pan.

In a medium bowl, cream well:
½ cup butter, softened
1 cup sugar
1 cup apricot preserves

Blend in:
½ cup buttermilk
3 large eggs

In a large bowl, sift together:
3 cups all-purpose flour
4 teaspoons baking powder
2 teaspoons baking soda
1 teaspoon *each* cinnamon, nutmeg, and cloves

Add:
2 cups cut-up dried apricots
Reserve:
2 cups fresh blueberries

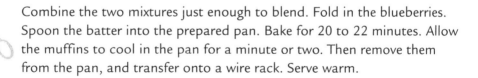

Combine the two mixtures just enough to blend. Fold in the blueberries. Spoon the batter into the prepared pan. Bake for 20 to 22 minutes. Allow the muffins to cool in the pan for a minute or two. Then remove them from the pan, and transfer onto a wire rack. Serve warm.

Apricot Orange Muffins

Laced with apricots, these luscious muffins are delicious served warm for dessert or tea.

Yield: 12 large muffins   Preheat the oven to 400°F and prepare the pan.

In a medium bowl, blend well:
2 large eggs
½ cup butter, melted and cooled
2 teaspoons vanilla extract
1 cup fresh orange juice
1 cup orange marmalade
   or apricot preserves, melted
1 tablespoon grated orange peel

In a large bowl, sift together:
3 cups all-purpose flour
1 cup sugar
4 teaspoons baking powder
1 teaspoon baking soda

Add:
2 cups cut-up dried apricots

Combine the two mixtures just enough to blend. Spoon the batter into the prepared pan. Bake for 20 minutes. Before removing the muffins from the pan, pour 1 tablespoon orange juice over the tops while they are still hot from the oven. Allow the juice to soak through; then transfer them onto a wire rack. Serve warm.

Variation

If you prefer, sprinkle tops generously with cinnamon sugar before baking. In a small bowl, blend ¼ cup granulated sugar, 2 teaspoons cinnamon, and ¼ teaspoon nutmeg. Omit the orange juice glaze.

Banana Muffins

The wonderful aroma and richness of sweet bananas is impossible to resist.

Yield: 12 large muffins   Preheat the oven to 400°F and prepare the pan.

In a medium bowl, cream well:
1 cup sugar
½ cup butter, softened

Blend in:
4 large eggs
1 tablespoon vanilla extract

Add:
2 cups mashed very ripe bananas

In a large bowl, sift together:
3 cups all-purpose flour
1 tablespoon baking soda
1 tablespoon baking powder
1 tablespoon nutmeg or allspice

Add:
2 cups chopped toasted walnuts
  or pecans

Combine the two mixtures just enough to blend. Spoon the batter into the prepared pan. Bake for 20 to 25 minutes. Remove the muffins from the pan, and cool on a wire rack. Serve warm.

Variations

Banana Butterscotch
Substitute 1 cup *each* butterscotch morsels and chopped pecans for the nuts. Substitute 1 cup packed brown sugar for the granulated sugar, and 1 tablespoon maple extract for the vanilla.

Banana Cornmeal
Substitute 1 cup yellow cornmeal for 1 cup flour.

More variations of . . . Banana Muffins

Cinnamon Banana
Substitute 1 tablespoon cinnamon for 1 tablespoon nutmeg or allspice. Sprinkle the tops with cinnamon-sugar topping before baking.

For the topping, mix ¼ cup granulated sugar, 2 teaspoons cinnamon, and ¼ teaspoon nutmeg.

Banana Cheese
Substitute 1 (8-oz.) package softened cream cheese for the butter.

White Chocolate–Banana
Add 1 cup chopped white chocolate and 1 cup shredded coconut to the dry ingredients.

Banana Carrot Muffins

Mildly sweet and nutty, these muffins are wonderful served with softened cream cheese.

Yield: 12 large muffins   Preheat the oven to 400°F and prepare the pan.

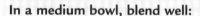

In a medium bowl, blend well:
4 large eggs
½ cup butter, melted and cooled
1 tablespoon vanilla extract

Add:
2 cups mashed very ripe bananas
1 cup shredded coconut
3 cups grated carrots

In a large bowl, sift together:
3½ cups all-purpose flour
1 tablespoon baking soda
1 tablespoon baking powder
1 cup packed brown sugar
1 tablespoon nutmeg
½ teaspoon *each* cloves and allspice

Add:
2 cups chopped walnuts

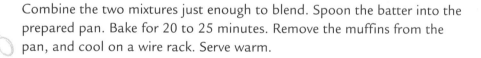

Combine the two mixtures just enough to blend. Spoon the batter into the prepared pan. Bake for 20 to 25 minutes. Remove the muffins from the pan, and cool on a wire rack. Serve warm.

Banana Coconut Muffins

A sweet breakfast muffin or a lush tea snack—serve it with poached fresh fruit.

Yield: 12 large muffins   Preheat the oven to 400°F and prepare the pan.

In a medium bowl, cream well:
½ cup butter, softened
1 cup packed brown sugar

Blend in:
4 large eggs
2 cups mashed very ripe bananas
1 tablespoon vanilla extract

In a large bowl, sift together:
3 cups all-purpose flour
1 tablespoon baking powder
1 tablespoon baking soda
1 teaspoon allspice
1 tablespoon nutmeg or cinnamon

Add:
1 (7-oz.) package coconut
1 cup mini–chocolate chips

Combine the two mixtures just enough to blend. Spoon the batter into the prepared pan. Bake for 20 to 25 minutes. Remove the muffins from the pan, and cool on a wire rack. Serve warm.

Variation

Banana Coconut Macadamia
Add 1 tablespoon grated lemon peel to the wet ingredients. Substitute 1 cup chopped unsalted macadamia nuts for the chocolate chips.

Banana Orange Muffins

Bananas and orange juice blend into a fragrant, sweet muffin made even more delicious served with warmed honey or maple syrup.

Yield: 12 large muffins   Preheat the oven to 400°F and prepare the pan.

In a medium bowl, blend well:
5 large eggs
½ cup butter, melted and cooled
¾ cup fresh orange juice
1 tablespoon orange
    or vanilla extract
1 tablespoon grated orange peel

Add:
1 cup mashed very ripe bananas

In a large bowl, sift together:
3½ cups all-purpose flour
½ teaspoon baking soda
2 tablespoons baking powder
1 cup packed brown sugar
1½ teaspoons *each* nutmeg and allspice

Add:
2 cups chopped walnuts or pecans

Combine the two mixtures just enough to blend. Spoon the batter into the prepared pan. Bake for 20 minutes. Remove the muffins from the pan, and cool on a wire rack. Serve warm.

Banana—Poppy Seed Muffins

Abundant with sweet bananas and poppy seeds, these muffins are perfect for brunch or dessert.

Yield: 12 large muffins   Preheat the oven to 400°F and prepare the pan.

In a medium bowl, cream well:
½ cup butter, softened
1 cup packed brown sugar

Blend in:
4 large eggs
1 tablespoon vanilla
  or banana extract
⅓ cup fresh orange juice

Add:
2½ cups mashed very ripe bananas

In a large bowl, sift together:
2 cups all-purpose flour
1½ cups whole-wheat flour,
  or all-purpose flour
2 tablespoons baking powder
½ teaspoon baking soda
1 tablespoon nutmeg

Add:
½ cup poppy seeds

Combine the two mixtures just enough to blend. Spoon the batter into the prepared pan. Bake for 20 to 25 minutes. Remove the muffins from the pan, and cool on a wire rack. Serve warm.

Variation

Raspberry Banana
Substitute 1½ cups oat bran for the whole-wheat flour, and 2 cups chopped toasted hazelnuts for the poppy seeds. After blending the batter, fold in 2 cups fresh raspberries. Bake as directed.

Banana Pumpkin Muffins

These are wonderful muffins to serve with a warm spiced fruit compote.

Yield: 12 large muffins

Preheat the oven to 375°F and prepare the pan.

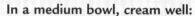

In a medium bowl, cream well:
1½ cups packed brown sugar
½ cup butter, softened

Blend in:
4 large eggs
1 tablespoon vanilla extract

Add:
1 cup mashed very ripe bananas
1 cup mashed fresh or canned
  solid-pack pumpkin
½ cup milk

In a large bowl, sift together:
3 cups all-purpose flour
1 tablespoon baking soda
1 tablespoon baking powder
1 tablespoon allspice

Add:
1 cup currants or cut-up pitted
  dates
2 cups chopped walnuts or pecans

Combine the two mixtures just enough to blend. Spoon the batter into the prepared pan. Bake for 25 minutes. Remove the muffins from the pan, and cool on a wire rack. Serve warm.

Variations

Banana Pumpkin-Pistachio
Substitute 1 cup chopped unsalted pistachio nuts for 1 cup walnuts.
Add 1 cup shredded coconut to the wet ingredients.

Tropical Papaya Spice
Substitute 2 cups mashed fresh ripe papaya for the pumpkin and the banana.

Black Walnut—Cranberry Muffins

Cranberries and black walnuts are native to the Americas. Cranberries add a tangy bite, while black walnuts offer a pungent, earthy flavor.

Yield: 12 large muffins   Preheat the oven to 400°F and prepare the pan.

In a medium bowl, blend well:
4 large eggs
½ cup butter, melted and cooled
½ cup milk
½ cup fresh orange juice
1 tablespoon vanilla extract
2 tablespoons grated orange peel
3 cups (12-oz. package) fresh
   cranberries

In a large bowl, sift together:
3 cups all-purpose flour
1½ cups sugar
2 tablespoons baking powder
1 teaspoon baking soda

Add:
2 cups black walnut pieces*

*Black walnuts may be purchased year-round by mail order from Sunnyland Farms and Missouri Dandy Pantry. See Appendix 2 for the addresses and phone numbers.

Combine the two mixtures just enough to blend. Fold in the cranberries. Spoon the batter into the prepared pan. Bake for 18 to 20 minutes. Remove the muffins from the pan, and cool on a wire rack. Serve warm.

Blueberry Muffins

These muffins, brimming with sweet blueberries, are jewels of the summer season—a perfect dessert served with pure vanilla ice cream.

Yield: 12 large muffins

Preheat the oven to 400°F and prepare the pan, using extra-large paper cups to line the muffin tin.

In a medium bowl, blend well:
5 large eggs
½ cup butter, melted and cooled
1 tablespoon vanilla extract
½ cup milk

In a large bowl, sift together:
3½ cups all-purpose flour
1 cup sugar
2 tablespoons baking powder
1 teaspoon baking soda
1 tablespoon cinnamon or nutmeg (optional)
Other ingredients:
4 cups fresh blueberries
1 cup mashed blueberries
Additional sugar

Combine the two mixtures just enough to blend. Fold in the blueberries. Spoon the batter into the prepared pan. Sprinkle generously with sugar.

Bake for 20 to 25 minutes. Remove the muffins from the pan, and cool on a wire rack. Serve warm.

Variations

Blueberry Raspberry
Substitute 2 cups fresh raspberries for 2 cups blueberries.

Blueberry Banana
Substitute 2 cups cut-up firm bananas for 2 cups blueberries. Add 1 cup chopped pecans to the dry ingredients.

Blackberry
Substitute 4 cups fresh blackberries for the blueberries.

Red Currant
Substitute 4 cups fresh red currants for the blueberries.

Butternut Squash Muffins

These muffins offer a snappy accompaniment to roast chicken or pork.

Yield: 12 large muffins   Preheat the oven to 375°F and prepare the pan.

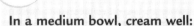

In a medium bowl, cream well:
½ cup butter, softened
1 cup packed brown sugar

Blend in:
4 large eggs
1 tablespoon grated orange peel
1 tablespoon vanilla extract

Add:
2 cups cooked butternut squash*
1 (8-oz.) can crushed pineapple
   in juice, undrained

In a large bowl, sift together:
3½ cups all-purpose flour
1 tablespoon baking powder
1 tablespoon baking soda
1 tablespoon cinnamon
½ teaspoon ginger
½ teaspoon allspice

Add:
2 cups chopped walnuts or unsalted,
   roasted cashews (optional)
1 cup raisins (optional)

*To cook squash: Preheat the oven to 400°F. Scrub a 3- to 4-lb. butternut squash. Place it on the middle rack and bake it until it can be pierced easily with a toothpick, about 1 hour. Cut it into quarters and remove the seeds. Peel the squash and mash the pulp. Look for squash that is firm with glossy skin and no brown patches. Avoid any that are overripe with a dull appearance.

Combine the two mixtures just enough to blend. Spoon the batter into the prepared pan. Bake for 25 minutes. Remove the muffins from the pan, and cool on a wire rack. Serve warm.

Carrot—Cream Cheese Muffins

With a rich center of cream cheese, these muffins are delicious served with butter flavored with honey or maple syrup.

Yield: 12 large muffins   Preheat the oven to 375°F and prepare the pan.

In a medium bowl, combine:
1 cup 100% bran cereal (not flakes)
½ cup boiling water

In a small bowl, blend until smooth: *
4 oz. cream cheese, softened
¼ cup sugar

*Prepare the filling before you start the muffin batter, so the muffins will be ready to go into the oven promptly.

In a large bowl, blend well:
2 large eggs
½ cup butter, melted and cooled
2 cups buttermilk

Add:
1 cup grated carrots
bran mixture

In a large bowl, sift together:
2½ cups all-purpose flour
½ cup granulated sugar
½ cup packed brown sugar
1 tablespoon baking soda
1 tablespoon cinnamon

Add:
2 cups rolled oats
1 cup chopped walnuts or pecans

Combine the two mixtures just enough to blend. Spoon half the batter into the prepared pan. Top with 1 tablespoon cream cheese filling, and then with the remaining batter. Bake for 18 to 20 minutes. Remove the muffins from the pan, and cool on a wire rack. Serve warm.

Cheesy Potato and Wild Rice Muffins

Potatoes deliver a delicate texture to these muffins. Serve with an omelet or salad.

Yield: 12 to 14 large muffins   Preheat the oven to 400°F and prepare the pan.

In a large bowl, blend well:
4 large eggs
½ cup butter, melted and cooled
1 cup buttermilk

Add:
½ cup chopped fresh chives
1 cup *each* finely chopped onion and
   celery
¼ cup chopped fresh parsley
2 cups cooked wild rice
2 cups grated cheese
2 cups mashed baked potato
   (not instant)

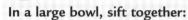

In a large bowl, sift together:
3 cups all-purpose flour
2 tablespoons baking powder
1 teaspoon baking soda

Combine the two mixtures just enough to blend. Spoon the batter into the prepared pan. Bake for 20 minutes. Remove the muffins from the pan, and cool on a wire rack. Serve warm.

Cherry Muffins

Sweet fruity muffins chock-full of fresh summer cherries and toasted almonds.

Yield: 12 large muffins   Preheat the oven to 425°F and prepare the pan.

In a medium bowl, blend well:
5 large eggs
½ cup butter, melted and cooled
1½ teaspoons *each* almond
    and vanilla extract
1 cup cherry or plain yogurt
1 tablespoon grated orange peel

In a large bowl, sift together:
3½ cups all-purpose flour
1 cup sugar
2 tablespoons baking powder
1 teaspoon baking soda
1 tablespoon cinnamon or nutmeg

Add:
2 cups slivered almonds, toasted

Keep aside:
4 cups pitted sweet cherries, halved

Combine the two mixtures just enough to blend. Fold in the cherries.
Spoon the batter into the prepared pan. Bake for 20 to 25 minutes.
Remove the muffins from the pan, and cool on a wire rack. Serve warm.

Variations

Chips and Cherry
Add 1 cup mini-chocolate chips to the dry ingredients.

More variations of . . . Cherry Muffins

Cherry-Almond Amaretto
While the muffins are still hot, and before removing them from the pan, pour 1 table-spoon Amaretto liqueur over the tops. Allow the Amaretto to soak through, then transfer them onto a wire rack. Serve warm.

Brandied Cherry
Soak cherries overnight in 1 to 1½ cups brandy. Drain well, and reserve any remaining brandy. Fold in cherries *after* the batter has been blended. Bake as directed. Before removing the muffins from the pan, pour 1 tablespoon reserved brandy over them while they're still hot. Allow the brandy to soak through, then transfer them onto a wire rack.

Cherry Fig
Substitute 2 cups cut-up dried figs for 2 cups cherries.

Cherry Chocolate
Add ⅓ cup unsweetened cocoa powder to the wet ingredients.

Coconut Carrot Muffins

These beauties are not to be missed!

Yield: 12 large muffins   Preheat the oven to 400°F and prepare the pan.

In a medium bowl, blend well:
4 large eggs
½ cup butter, melted and cooled
1 tablespoon grated orange peel
2 teaspoons vanilla extract

Add:
3 cups grated carrots
1 (8-oz.) can crushed pineapple
   in juice, undrained
1 cup shredded coconut

*You may substitute 1 cup cut-up dried apricots, pitted dates, or pitted prunes for the raisins.

In a large bowl, sift together:
3½ cups all-purpose flour
1 cup sugar
1 tablespoon baking soda
1 tablespoon baking powder
1 tablespoon cinnamon
½ teaspoon ginger
¼ teaspoon *each* nutmeg, cloves,
   and allspice

Add:
1 cup sliced bananas (optional)
1 cup chopped walnuts, pecans,
   or slivered almonds
1 cup raisins*
½ cup mini–chocolate chips
(optional)

Combine the two mixtures just enough to blend. Spoon the batter into the prepared pan. Bake for 20 to 25 minutes. Remove the muffins from the pan, and cool on a wire rack. Serve warm.

Cranberry Nut Muffins

Sweetened with a twist of orange, these muffins lend the perfect touch to holiday feasts. Or serve them for breakfast with fresh jams and preserves.

Yield: 12 large muffins   Preheat the oven to 425°F and prepare the pan.

In a medium bowl, blend well:
2 large eggs
½ cup butter, melted and cooled
1 tablespoon vanilla
    or almond extract
1 cup sour cream
1 cup fresh orange juice
1 tablespoon grated orange peel

Other ingredients:
3 cups (12-oz. package)
    fresh cranberries
Additional sugar for topping

In a large bowl, sift together:
3½ cups all-purpose flour
1½ cups sugar
2 tablespoons baking powder
1 teaspoon baking soda
1 tablespoon cinnamon or nutmeg

Add:
2 cups chopped walnuts, pecans,
    or slivered almonds
1 cup mini–chocolate chips
(optional)

Combine the two mixtures just enough to blend. Fold in the cranberries. Spoon the batter into the prepared pan. Sprinkle generously with sugar. Bake for 20 to 25 minutes. Remove the muffins from the pan, and cool on a wire rack. Serve warm.

Variation

Apricot Cranberry
Omit the chocolate chips. Add 1 cup cut-up dried apricots to the dry ingredients.

Date Banana Muffins

This recipe makes a sweet breakfast or tea muffin to serve with spiced cider or orange tea.

Yield: 12 large muffins   Preheat the oven to 400°F and prepare the pan.

In a medium bowl, cream well:
½ cup butter, softened
1 cup packed brown sugar

Blend in:
4 large eggs
1 tablespoon vanilla extract
1 cup buttermilk
2 cups mashed very ripe bananas

In a large bowl, sift together:
3 cups all-purpose flour
1 tablespoon baking powder
1 tablespoon baking soda
2 teaspoons cinnamon
1 teaspoon cloves

Add:
2 cups rolled oats
2 cups chopped pecans or walnuts
2 cups cut-up pitted dates

 Combine the two mixtures just enough to blend. Spoon the batter into the prepared pan. Bake for 22 to 25 minutes. Remove the muffins from the pan, and cool on a wire rack. Serve warm.

Date Nut Muffins

The dates give these muffins a wonderful, rich flavor. They are delicious with sweet butter or cream cheese.

Yield: 12 large muffins   Preheat the oven to 400°F and prepare the pan.

In a medium bowl, blend well:
4 large eggs
½ cup butter, melted and cooled
1 tablespoon vanilla extract
2 cups sour cream

In a large bowl, sift together:
3½ cups all-purpose flour
1 cup packed brown sugar
2 tablespoons baking powder
1 teaspoon baking soda
1 tablespoon cinnamon
¼ teaspoon *each* cloves, nutmeg, and allspice

Add:
1½ cups cut-up pitted dates
1 cup chopped walnuts or pecans

Combine the two mixtures just enough to blend. Spoon the batter into the prepared pan. Bake for 20 minutes. Remove the muffins from the pan, and cool on a wire rack. Serve warm.

Variations

Chocolate–Date Nut
With the dry ingredients, sift together 3 tablespoons instant espresso or coffee powder and ½ cup unsweetened cocoa powder.

Honey–Date Nut
Omit the brown sugar. Substitute 1 cup honey for 1 cup sour cream. Reduce temperature to 375°F.

Fresh Grapefruit Muffins

These tangy, extra-light muffins are especially good topped with sweet marmalade.

Yield: 10 large muffins   Preheat the oven to 400°F and prepare the pan.

In a medium bowl, cream well:
½ cup butter, softened
1 cup sugar

Blend in:
4 large eggs
1 tablespoon vanilla extract
¾ cup fresh grapefruit juice
¾ cup milk
2 tablespoons grated grapefruit peel

In a large bowl, sift together:
3 cups all-purpose flour
2 tablespoons baking powder
½ teaspoon baking soda
1 tablespoon cinnamon

Combine the two mixtures just enough to blend. Spoon the batter into the prepared pan. Bake for 20 minutes. Remove the muffins from the pan, and cool on a wire rack. Serve warm.

Variations

Tangerine Walnut
Substitute ¾ cup fresh tangerine juice for the grapefruit juice and 2 tablespoons grated tangerine peel for the grapefruit peel. Add 1 cup finely chopped walnuts to the dry ingredients.

Apple Cider
Substitute ¾ cup apple (or pear) cider for the grapefruit juice and 2 tablespoons grated orange peel for the grapefruit peel. Add ½ teaspoon mace and 1 cup finely chopped walnuts or pecans to the dry ingredients.

Honey Curry Muffins

The spunky flavor of curry creates a delicious muffin to serve with a variety of main-course salads.

Yield: 12 large muffins   Preheat the oven to 375°F and prepare the pan.

In a medium bowl, blend well:
3 large eggs
½ cup butter, melted and cooled
1 cup honey

Add:
1 cup finely chopped onion
1 cup grated apple
1 cup grated unpeeled zucchini

In a large bowl, sift together:
3 cups all-purpose flour
1 tablespoon baking powder
1 tablespoon baking soda
2 tablespoons curry powder

Add:
1 cup slivered almonds

Combine the two mixtures just enough to blend. Spoon the batter into the prepared pan. Bake for 20 minutes. Remove the muffins from the pan, and cool on a wire rack. Serve warm.

Honey Oat–Prune Muffins

These muffins are a splendid accompaniment to a simple meal of fresh fruit and yogurt.

Yield: 12 large muffins   Preheat the oven to 375°F and prepare the pan.

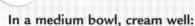

In a medium bowl, cream well:
½ cup butter, softened
½ cup packed brown sugar
½ cup honey

Blend in:
2 large eggs
1 teaspoon vanilla extract
orange juice–prune mixture*
   (2 cups fresh orange juice
   and 2 cups cut-up pitted prunes)

In a large bowl, sift together:
3 cups all-purpose flour
1 tablespoon baking powder

Add:
2 cups rolled oats
½ cup wheat germ
2 cups chopped walnuts or pecans

*Using an electric blender, blend the orange juice
and prunes until the mixture is almost smooth,
then blend with the rest of the wet ingredients.

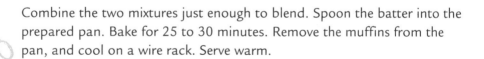

Combine the two mixtures just enough to blend. Spoon the batter into the prepared pan. Bake for 25 to 30 minutes. Remove the muffins from the pan, and cool on a wire rack. Serve warm.

Jalapeño Beer Muffins

These muffins are perfect served with creamy butter and bowls of chili.

Yield: 10 large muffins   Preheat the oven to 400°F and prepare the pan.

In a medium bowl, blend well:
3 large eggs
1 (12-oz.) can lager beer,
  at room temperature

Add:
1 to 2 cups finely chopped jalapeño
  peppers, or 1 to 2 (4.5-oz.) cans
  chopped green chilies, drained

In a large bowl, sift together:
3 cups all-purpose flour
1 tablespoon baking powder
1 tablespoon baking soda

Cut in:
1 cup shortening
Blend until mixture resembles coarse
meal.

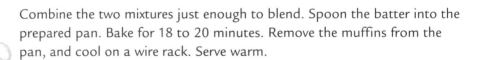

Combine the two mixtures just enough to blend. Spoon the batter into the prepared pan. Bake for 18 to 20 minutes. Remove the muffins from the pan, and cool on a wire rack. Serve warm.

Lemon Orange Muffins

Fresh berries and peaches, with just a sprinkle of sugar, deliciously complement these citrus-flavored muffins.

Yield: 11 large muffins   Preheat the oven to 400°F and prepare the pan.

In a medium bowl, blend well:
4 large eggs
½ cup butter, melted and cooled
½ cup *each* fresh lemon juice
   and orange juice
1 tablespoon *each* grated lemon peel
   and orange peel
1 tablespoon lemon, orange,
   or vanilla extract

In a large bowl, sift together:
3½ cups all-purpose flour
1 cup packed brown sugar
2 tablespoons baking powder
1 teaspoon baking soda
1 teaspoon *each* cinnamon and
allspice
¼ teaspoon *each* cloves and nutmeg

Hold:
1 (15-oz.) can mandarin orange
   sections, drained

Combine the two mixtures just enough to blend. Fold in the mandarin orange sections. Spoon the batter into the prepared pan. Bake for 20 to 25 minutes. Remove the muffins from the pan, and cool on a wire rack. Serve warm.

Variations

Lemon Orange–Ginger
Add ½ cup peeled, grated fresh ginger to the wet ingredients.

Lemon Orange–Pecan
Add 2 cups chopped pecans to the dry ingredients.

Olive Muffins

Kalamata olives are from Greece. You may also use Nicoise olives if you prefer. Canned American olives do not have the flavor or pungency needed for this recipe.

Yield: 12 large muffins   Preheat the oven to 400°F and prepare the pan.

In a large bowl, blend well:
5 large eggs
½ cup butter, melted and cooled
2 cups sour cream or milk

Add:
1 cup chopped, pitted Kalamata
   or other brine-cured black olives
1 cup chopped, pitted large
   green olives

In a large bowl, sift together:
3½ cups all-purpose flour
2 tablespoons baking powder
½ teaspoon baking soda

Combine the two mixtures just enough to blend. Spoon the batter into the prepared pan. Bake for 20 to 25 minutes. Remove the muffins from the pan, and cool on a wire rack. Serve warm.

Variation

Olive Mint
Omit 1 cup green olives. Add 1 cup chopped fresh mint leaves and 1 cup grated onion to the wet ingredients.

Orange and Sweet Parsnip Muffins

Try these as an accompaniment to roast pork.

Yield: 12 large muffins   Preheat the oven to 400°F and prepare the pan.

In a large bowl, blend well:
4 large eggs
½ cup butter, melted and cooled
¾ cup fresh orange juice
1 tablespoon vanilla extract
1 cup sour cream or plain yogurt

Add:
3 cups grated parsnips
2 tablespoons grated orange peel
1 (7-oz.) package coconut

In a large bowl, sift together:
3½ cups all-purpose flour
1 cup sugar
1 tablespoon baking soda
1 tablespoon baking powder
1 tablespoon cinnamon
½ teaspoon cloves

Add:
1 cup chopped walnuts or pecans
  (optional)
½ cup raisins (optional)

Combine the two mixtures just enough to blend. Spoon the batter into the prepared pan. Bake for 20 minutes. Remove the muffins from the pan, and cool on a wire rack. Serve warm.

Pineapple Apricot Muffins

Crushed pineapple adds a refreshing sweetness to these apricot muffins.

Yield: 12 large muffins   Preheat the oven to 400°F and prepare the pan.

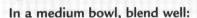

In a medium bowl, blend well:
4 large eggs
½ cup butter, melted and cooled
1 tablespoon vanilla extract
1 cup pineapple or apricot yogurt
1 tablespoon grated orange peel

Add:
1 (8-oz.) can crushed pineapple
   in juice, undrained

In a large bowl, sift together:
3½ cups all-purpose flour
2 tablespoons baking powder
1 teaspoon baking soda
1 cup sugar
1 tablespoon nutmeg

Add:
1 cup chopped pecans, walnuts,
   or hazelnuts
2 cups cut-up dried apricots

Combine the two mixtures just enough to blend. Spoon the batter into the prepared pan. Bake for 20 to 25 minutes. Remove the muffins from the pan, and cool on a wire rack. Serve warm.

Variation

Pineapple Apricot–Coconut
Add 1 cup shredded coconut to the wet ingredients.

Pineapple Zucchini Muffins

Tangy pineapple, coconut, and pecans accent these muffins.

Yield: 12 large muffins

Preheat the oven to 400°F and prepare the pan.

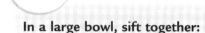

In a large bowl, blend well:
3 large eggs
½ cup butter, melted and cooled
1 tablespoon vanilla extract

Add:
2 to 3 cups grated unpeeled zucchini
1 (8-oz.) can crushed pineapple
   in juice
1 cup shredded coconut
1 tablespoon grated lemon peel

In a large bowl, sift together:
3 cups all-purpose flour
1 tablespoon baking powder
1 tablespoon baking soda
2 tablespoons cinnamon
1 cup sugar

Add:
2 cups chopped pecans or walnuts
½ cup raisins

Combine the two mixtures just enough to blend. Spoon the batter into the prepared pan. Bake for 20 minutes. Remove the muffins from the pan, and cool on a wire rack. Serve warm.

Pistachio Apricot Muffins

These are delicious served with jams or fruit preserves. Or drizzle them with honey for a rich, velvety flavor.

Yield: 12 large muffins   Preheat the oven to 375°F and prepare the pan.

In a large bowl, blend well:
5 large eggs
½ cup butter, melted and cooled
1 cup honey
1 tablespoon vanilla
  or almond extract
2 tablespoons grated orange peel
2 cups low-fat cottage cheese
½ cup sour cream or plain yogurt

In a large bowl, sift together:
3½ cups all-purpose flour
4 teaspoons baking powder
1 tablespoon baking soda
1 tablespoon nutmeg

Add:
1 cup chopped pistachio nuts, unsalted
1 cup cut-up dried apricots
½ cup dark raisins

 Combine the two mixtures just enough to blend. Spoon the batter into the prepared pan. Bake for 18 to 20 minutes. Remove the muffins from the pan, and cool on a wire rack. Serve warm.

Variation
Pistachio Fig
Substitute 1 cup cut-up dried figs for the apricots.

Pumpkin Curry Muffins

Pumpkin muffins with just enough snap to warm a winter meal.

Yield: 12 large muffins

Preheat the oven to 400°F and prepare the pan.

Onion Mixture:

2 tablespoons butter
1½ cups finely chopped onion
2 tablespoons curry powder
½ teaspoon ground cumin
⅛ teaspoon cayenne pepper

In a skillet over medium heat, melt the butter and add the onion, curry powder, cumin, and cayenne pepper. Sauté onions until soft, about 5 minutes. Set aside to cool.

In a large bowl, blend well:

3 large eggs
¼ cup butter, melted and cooled
1 cup buttermilk

Add:

Onion mixture
1 (16-oz.) can solid-pack pumpkin

In a large bowl, sift together:

2 cups all-purpose flour
2 tablespoons baking powder
1 teaspoon baking soda

Add:

2 cups yellow cornmeal

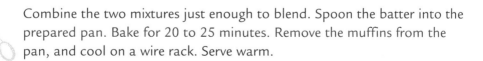

Combine the two mixtures just enough to blend. Spoon the batter into the prepared pan. Bake for 20 to 25 minutes. Remove the muffins from the pan, and cool on a wire rack. Serve warm.

Pumpkin Muffins

Traditionally, pumpkin is a fall season favorite; but there's no need to wait to savor its special flavor.

Yield: 12 large muffins   Preheat the oven to 375°F and prepare the pan.

In a medium bowl, cream well:
1½ cups packed brown sugar
½ cup butter, softened

Blend in:
4 large eggs
1 tablespoon vanilla or maple extract

Add:
2 cups mashed fresh
  or canned solid-pack pumpkin
½ cup milk

In a large bowl, sift together:
3 cups all-purpose flour
1 tablespoon baking powder
1 tablespoon baking soda
1 teaspoon *each* cinnamon and nutmeg
1 teaspoon *each* ginger and allspice
¼ teaspoon cloves

Add:
2 cups chopped pecans or walnuts
1 cup raisins (optional)

Combine the two mixtures just enough to blend. Spoon the batter into the prepared pan. Bake for 25 minutes. Remove the muffins from the pan, and cool on a wire rack. Serve warm.

Variations

Pumpkin Oatmeal
Substitute 1½ cups rolled oats for 1½ cups all-purpose flour.

Pumpkin Whole-Wheat
Substitute 1½ cups whole-wheat flour for 1½ cups all-purpose flour
and 1 cup cut-up pitted prunes or dates for the raisins.

More variations of . . . Pumpkin Muffins

Pumpkin Orange
Substitute ½ cup fresh orange juice for the milk, and add 1 tablespoon grated orange peel to the wet ingredients.

Apricot Pumpkin
Substitute 1 cup toasted pumpkin seeds or slivered almonds for 1 cup pecans, and 1 cup cut-up dried apricots for the raisins.

Cornmeal Pumpkin
Substitute 1½ cups yellow cornmeal for 1½ cups all-purpose flour.

Pumpkin–Chocolate Chip
Add 2 cups mini–chocolate chips to the dry ingredients. Omit the raisins and nuts.

Sour Cream–Pumpkin
Add 1 cup sour cream to the wet ingredients, and omit the milk.

Cranberry Pumpkin
Omit the raisins. After blending the batter, fold in 3 cups (12-oz. package) fresh cranberries.

Pumpkin Cider
Add 1 cup apple cider and 2 tablespoons grated orange peel to the wet ingredients. Omit the milk.

Rhubarb Muffins

Offer these muffins with strawberry preserves. Fresh, tender rhubarb is available only in the early spring, so try these while you can. Frozen rhubarb works equally well.

Yield: 12 large muffins   Preheat the oven to 400°F and prepare the pan.

In a medium bowl, combine:
3 cups diced fresh rhubarb stalks,
   or 1 (20-oz.) bag frozen, thawed,
   and drained
⅔ cup sugar
Let stand 30 minutes, stirring occasionally, reserve.

In a large bowl, sift together:
3½ cups all-purpose flour
2 tablespoons baking powder
1 teaspoon allspice

Add:
2 cups chopped pecans or walnuts

Combine the two mixtures, not the rhubarb, just enough to blend. Fold in the rhubarb. Spoon the batter into the prepared pan.

In a small bowl, mix ½ cup granulated sugar, 4 teaspoons cinnamon, and ½ teaspoon nutmeg. Sprinkle the tops generously with this Cinnamon Sugar, keeping any leftover for another use.

In a blender, mix well:
2 large eggs
1 cup pure maple syrup
½ cup butter, softened
1 cup milk
1 tablespoon vanilla extract

Bake for 25 minutes. Remove the muffins from the pan, and cool on a wire rack. Serve warm.

Variations

Cherry Rhubarb
Fold in 2 cups pitted, halved tart cherries along with the rhubarb.

Rhubarb Cranberry
Fold in 3 cups (12-oz. package) fresh cranberries, *after* the batter has been blended.

Sour Cream–Peach Muffins

Kissed with juicy peaches and fragrant spices, these muffins are one of summer's special treats. Serve with raspberry preserves or vanilla ice cream.

Yield: 12 large muffins   Preheat the oven to 400°F and prepare the pan.

In a medium bowl, cream well:
½ cup butter, softened
1 cup packed brown sugar

Blend in:
4 large eggs
1½ teaspoons *each* vanilla
    and almond extract
½ cup sour cream
2 cups mashed very ripe peaches

In a large bowl, sift together:
3 cups all-purpose flour
4 teaspoons baking powder
2 teaspoons baking soda
1 tablespoon cinnamon or allspice
1 teaspoon cardamom

Add:
1 cup chopped pecans
    or sliced almonds

Combine the two mixtures just enough to blend. Spoon the batter into the prepared pan.

In a small bowl, mix ½ cup granulated sugar, 4 teaspoons cinnamon, and ½ teaspoon nutmeg. Sprinkle the tops generously with this Cinnamon Sugar, keeping any leftover for another use.

Bake for 25 minutes. Remove the muffins from the pan, and cool on a wire rack. Serve warm.

Variations

Peach Raspberry
After blending the batter, fold in 2 cups fresh raspberries.

Ginger Pear
Substitute 2 cups mashed very ripe pears for the peaches, and 1 cup currants for the nuts. Add ½ cup grated fresh ginger to the wet ingredients.

Sour Cream—Prune Muffins

Prunes provide succulent sweetness to these cinnamon scented muffins.

Yield: 12 large muffins   Preheat the oven to 400°F and prepare the pan.

In a medium bowl, blend well:
3 large eggs
½ cup butter, melted and cooled
2 cups sour cream or plain yogurt
2 teaspoons vanilla extract
¼ cup milk

In a large bowl, sift together:
3½ cups all-purpose flour
1½ cups sugar
4 teaspoons baking powder
2 teaspoons baking soda

Add:
2 cups cut-up pitted prunes
1 cup chopped walnuts

Combine the two mixtures just enough to blend. Spoon the batter into the prepared pan.

In a small bowl, mix ½ cup granulated sugar, 4 teaspoons cinnamon, and ½ teaspoon nutmeg. Sprinkle the tops generously with this Cinnamon Sugar, keeping any leftover for another use.

Bake for 25 minutes. Remove the muffins from the pan, and cool on a wire rack. Serve warm.

Variations

Apricot Prune
Sift 1 tablespoon cinnamon with the dry ingredients. Substitute 1 cup cut-up dried apricots for 1 cup prunes.

Apricot Prune–Chocolate Chip
Prepare Apricot Prune Muffins as directed. Substitute 1 cup mini-chocolate chips for 1 cup walnuts.

Sweet Morning Muffins

Great anytime, these sweet treats provide lots of happy munching.

Yield: 12 large muffins   Preheat the oven to 400°F and prepare the pan.

In a large bowl, blend well:
4 large eggs
½ cup butter, melted and cooled
1 tablespoons vanilla extract
1 cup plain yogurt

Add:
1½ cups *each* grated carrots
    and tart green apples
1 cup shredded coconut
1 tablespoon grated orange peel

In a large bowl, sift together:
3 cups all-purpose flour
2 tablespoons baking powder
1 cup packed brown sugar
1 tablespoon cinnamon or nutmeg
½ teaspoon ground cardamom

Add:
1 cup raisins
1 cup slivered almonds
1 cup rolled oats

Combine the two mixtures just enough to blend. Spoon the batter into the prepared pan. Bake for 20 to 25 minutes. Remove the muffins from the pan, and cool on a wire rack. Serve warm.

Variation

Carrot-Apple-Date
Substitute 1 cup cut-up pitted dates for the raisins, and 1 cup chopped macadamia nuts for the almonds.

Sweet Potato Muffins

A Southern favorite at holiday dinners, these muffins are particularly tasty with roast duck or chicken, and baked ham.

Yield: 12 large muffins   Preheat the oven to 375°F and prepare the pan.

In a medium bowl, cream well:
1½ cups packed brown sugar
½ cup butter, softened

Blend in:
4 large eggs
1 tablespoon vanilla extract
1 tablespoon grated orange peel

Add:
2 cups mashed baked sweet potato
½ cup milk

In a large bowl, sift together:
3 cups all-purpose flour
1 tablespoon baking powder
1 tablespoon baking soda
½ teaspoon cloves
1 teaspoon *each* nutmeg, allspice, and cinnamon

Add:
2 cups chopped walnuts or pecans

Combine the two mixtures just enough to blend. Spoon the batter into the prepared pan. Bake for 25 minutes. Remove the muffins from the pan, and cool on a wire rack. Serve warm.

Variations

Sweet Potato–Orange
Substitute ½ cup fresh orange juice for the milk. Add 1 cup cut-up pitted dates to the dry ingredients.

Sweet Potato–Banana
Substitute 1 cup mashed very ripe banana for 1 cup sweet potato. Add 1 cup shredded coconut to the wet ingredients.

Sweet Potato–Maple Walnut
Cut brown sugar to ½ cup, and add 1 cup pure maple syrup to the wet ingredients. Omit the milk.

Sweet Potato–Apricot
Add 1 cup apricot nectar to the wet ingredients. Omit the milk. Add 1 cup cut-up dried apricots to the dry ingredients.

Sweet Potato—Applesauce Muffins

Serve these muffins with mugs of hot spicy cider.

Yield: 12 large muffins

Preheat the oven to 400°F and prepare the pan.

In a medium bowl, blend well:
4 large eggs
½ cup butter, melted and cooled
1 tablespoon grated orange peel
1 tablespoon vanilla extract

Add:
2 cups grated, peeled raw
   sweet potato
2 cups unsweetened applesauce

In a large bowl, sift together:
2½ cups all-purpose flour
1 cup packed brown sugar
2 tablespoons baking powder
1 teaspoon baking soda
1 tablespoon allspice
½ teaspoon *each* cinnamon and
   nutmeg

Add:
½ cup wheat germ
½ cup oat bran
1 cup rolled oats
1 cup cut-up pitted prunes or dates
1 cup slivered almonds

 Combine the two mixtures just enough to blend. Spoon the batter into the prepared pan. Bake for 20 to 22 minutes. Remove the muffins from the pan, and cool on a wire rack. Serve warm.

Sweet Potato—Pepper Muffins

A marvelous joining of sweet and spicy flavors, these muffins are especially good with maple or fruit butters.

Yield: 10 large muffins   Preheat the oven to 350°F and prepare the pan.

In a medium bowl, blend well:
3 large eggs
½ cup butter, melted and cooled
½ cup milk

Add:
2 cups mashed baked sweet potato

In a large bowl, sift together:
3 cups all-purpose flour
1 cup sugar
1 tablespoon baking powder
1 tablespoon baking soda
2 to 3 tablespoons cracked
    black pepper

Combine the two mixtures just enough to blend. Spoon the batter into the prepared pan. Bake for 20 to 25 minutes. Remove the muffins from the pan, and cool on a wire rack. Serve warm.

Tropical Paradise Muffins

The lushness of the islands is packed into an exotic bit of indulgence.

Yield: 12 large muffins   Preheat the oven to 400°F and prepare the pan.

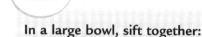

In a large bowl, blend well:
3 large eggs
½ cup butter, melted and cooled
1 tablespoon vanilla
  or coconut extract

Add:
1 cup mashed very ripe bananas
1 cup mashed ripe papaya
  or mango
1 (8-oz.) can crushed pineapple
  in juice, undrained
1 tablespoon grated lemon peel

In a large bowl, sift together:
3 cups all-purpose flour
1 cup packed light brown sugar
1 tablespoon baking powder
1 tablespoon baking soda
1 tablespoon nutmeg

Add:
1 cup rolled oats
1 cup shredded coconut
½ cup mini-chocolate chips
1 cup chopped toasted pecans
  or macadamia nuts

Combine the two mixtures just enough to blend. Spoon the batter into the prepared pan. Sprinkle tops generously with the Cinnamon Sugar* (optional), keeping any leftover for another use. Bake for 20 to 25 minutes. Remove the muffins from the pan, and cool on a wire rack. Serve warm.

*In a small bowl, mix ½ cup granulated sugar, 4 teaspoons cinnamon, and ½ teaspoon nutmeg.

Whole-Wheat Honey Banana Muffins

These banana muffins are graced with honey's subtle, sweet flavor.

Yield: 12 large muffins   Preheat the oven to 375°F and prepare the pan.

In a medium bowl, cream well:
½ cup butter, softened
¼ cup sugar

Blend in:
4 large eggs
¾ cup honey
1 tablespoon vanilla extract

Add:
2 cups mashed very ripe bananas

In a large bowl, sift together:
3 cups whole-wheat flour
1 tablespoon baking soda
1 tablespoon baking powder
1 tablespoon nutmeg or cinnamon

Add:
2 cups chopped pecans

Combine the two mixtures just enough to blend. Spoon the batter into the prepared pan. Bake for 20 to 25 minutes. Remove the muffins from the pan, and cool on a wire rack. Serve warm.

Variation

Banana–Maple Walnut
Substitute ¾ cup pure maple syrup for the honey, 3 cups all-purpose flour for the whole-wheat flour, and 2 cups chopped walnuts for the pecans.

Zucchini Herb Muffins

Served warm with a salad of fresh garden tomatoes, these make a simple, tasty summer lunch.

Yield: 12 large muffins   Preheat the oven to 400°F and prepare the pan.

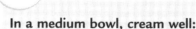

In a medium bowl, cream well:
½ cup butter, softened
¼ cup sugar

Blend in:
4 large eggs
1 cup buttermilk or plain yogurt

Add:
3 cups grated unpeeled zucchini
1½ cups finely chopped
   fresh basil leaves

In a large bowl, sift together:
3½ cups all-purpose flour
2 teaspoons baking soda
4 teaspoons baking powder
1 tablespoon ground black pepper

Combine the two mixtures just enough to blend. Spoon the batter into the prepared pan. Bake for 20 to 25 minutes. Remove the muffins from the pan, and cool on a wire rack. Serve warm.

Zucchini Spice Muffins

These muffins are a delicious way to use zucchini from an overflowing garden. Grate zucchini, wrap it in 2-cup packages, and freeze it so you can make these throughout the winter. They're a natural to serve with cream cheese.

Yield: 12 large muffins · Preheat the oven to 400°F and prepare the pan.

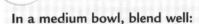

In a medium bowl, blend well:
3 large eggs
½ cup butter, melted and cooled
1 tablespoon vanilla extract
1 cup plain yogurt

Add:
2 to 3 cups grated
 unpeeled zucchini

In a large bowl, sift together:
3 cups all-purpose flour
1 cup packed brown sugar
1 tablespoon baking soda
1 tablespoon baking powder
1 tablespoon nutmeg or cinnamon
½ teaspoon cloves

Add:
1 cup chopped pecans, almonds,
 or walnuts
1 cup raisins

Combine the two mixtures just enough to blend. Spoon the batter into the prepared pan. Bake for 20 minutes. Remove the muffins from the pan, and cool on a wire rack. Serve warm.

Variations

Zucchini Ricotta
Substitute 1 cup ricotta cheese for the yogurt.

Chocolate Zucchini
Add ⅓ cup unsweetened cocoa powder and 1 tablespoon grated orange peel to the wet ingredients. Substitute 1 cup mini–chocolate chips for the raisins or nuts (optional).

Chapter 8

Cheese Muffins

Hundreds of types of cheeses are made all over the world, and their individual flavors and textures blend beautifully with the muffin recipes found here. Colby or Cheddar cheese can be combined with pasta to make simple Macaroni and Cheese Muffins that will be a favorite with both children and adults. Roquefort and blue cheese lend tang to vegetable muffins. Parmesan or Romano cheese, grated and blended into the batter or sprinkled over the top before baking, adds a zest that is incomparable. Fresh ricotta, cottage, and cream cheeses give smoothness and body to make rich-tasting muffins—as do any soft or aged cheeses.

Natural cheeses come in more than four hundred varieties. Their textures range from very hard and granular to creamy and soft—from Romano to Cheddar to Brie. And their flavors vary from mild cream cheese to nippy Swiss to pungent Limburger. A rich source of protein, vitamins, calcium, and other minerals, cheese finds a welcome place in our diets. Specialty shops and well-stocked supermarkets usually carry a large assortment of both imported and domestic brands. In a market's top-notch cheese shop where the turnover is high, select only wrapped cheeses kept in chilled cases, and read the label carefully to check the contents. Determine freshness, too, by sampling cheese whenever possible. In specialty stores where cheeses are cut from large wheels and blocks, customers are usually permitted to sample the wares. Take advantage of this opportunity to be sure the cheese you are considering is of peak quality.

Cheese muffins lend themselves to almost any occasion. They are ideal for children's snacks, a last-minute gathering, and even as dessert served with fruits and nuts.

Apple Cheese Muffins

The creamy texture of ricotta cheese creates rich, tender muffins.

Yield: 12 large muffins   Preheat the oven to 400°F and prepare the pan.

In a large bowl, blend well:
4 large eggs
½ cup butter, melted and cooled
¾ cup milk
1½ teaspoons *each* almond
    and vanilla extract

Add:
2 cups peeled, grated apples
2 cups ricotta cheese
2 cups grated Muenster cheese

In a large bowl, sift together:
3½ cups all-purpose flour
1 cup sugar
1 tablespoon baking soda
1 tablespoon baking powder
½ teaspoon nutmeg
2 teaspoons cinnamon

Add:
2 cups chopped walnuts or almonds

Combine the two mixtures just enough to blend. Spoon the batter into the prepared pan. Bake for 20 to 25 minutes. Remove the muffins from the pan, and cool on a wire rack. Serve warm.

Artichoke Cheddar Muffins

These will become a favorite to serve for a special dinner.

Yield: 12 large muffins   Preheat the oven to 400°F and prepare the pan.

In a large bowl, blend well:
3 large eggs
½ cup butter, melted and cooled
2 cups buttermilk

Add:
3 cups grated sharp Cheddar cheese
2 (14-oz.) cans artichoke hearts,
   drained and quartered
1 cup finely chopped scallions

In a large bowl, sift together:
3½ cups all-purpose flour
2 tablespoons baking powder
1 teaspoon baking soda

Add:
2 cups slivered almonds

Combine the two mixtures just enough to blend. Spoon the batter into the prepared pan. Bake for 22 to 25 minutes. Remove the muffins from the pan, and cool on a wire rack. Serve warm.

Blueberry Cheese Muffins

The mild flavor of the Lorraine cheese plays up the slightly sassy blueberries.

Yield: 12 large muffins   Preheat the oven to 400°F and prepare the pan.

In a medium bowl, cream well:
½ cup butter, softened
1 cup packed light brown sugar

Blend in:
2 large eggs
1 cup buttermilk
1 cup sour cream
2 teaspoons vanilla extract

Add:
2 cups grated Swiss Lorraine cheese

In a large bowl, sift together:
3 cups all-purpose flour
1 tablespoon baking powder
1 tablespoon baking soda

Reserve:
2 cups fresh blueberries

Combine the two mixtures just enough to blend. Fold in the blueberries. Spoon the batter into the prepared pan. Generously sprinkle the tops with Cinnamon Sugar, keeping any leftover for another use (optional).* Bake for 20 to 25 minutes. Remove the muffins from the pan, and transfer onto a wire rack. Serve warm.

*In a small bowl, mix ½ cup granulated sugar, 4 teaspoons cinnamon, and ½ teaspoon nutmeg.

Broccoli and Cauliflower Cheese Muffins

Serve with a rich homemade soup or stew.

Yield: 12 to 14 large muffins

Preheat the oven to 425°F
and prepare the pan.

In a large bowl, blend well:
3 large eggs
1/2 cup butter, melted and cooled

Add:
1 cup low-fat cottage cheese or milk
2 cups grated Cheddar
  or mozzarella cheese
1 cup *each* finely chopped onions,
  celery, and mushrooms
1 (10-oz.) package frozen chopped
  broccoli, thawed and well drained
1 (10-oz.) package frozen chopped
  cauliflower, thawed and well
  drained
2 cups cooked wild rice
1/2 cup minced fresh parsley
1 tablespoon oregano

In a large bowl, sift together:
3 cups all-purpose flour
2 tablespoons baking powder
1/2 teaspoon baking soda
1 tablespoon ground black pepper

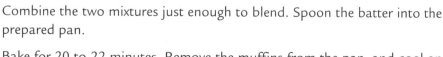

Combine the two mixtures just enough to blend. Spoon the batter into the prepared pan.

Bake for 20 to 22 minutes. Remove the muffins from the pan, and cool on a wire rack. Serve warm.

Caraway Cheddar Muffins

These muffins are ideal accompaniments to baked ham, fresh turkey, and thick soups.

Yield: 12 large muffins   Preheat the oven to 425°F and prepare the pan.

In a large bowl, blend well:

2 large eggs
½ cup butter, melted and cooled
1 cup sour cream
1 cup milk
1 tablespoon Worcestershire sauce

Add:

4 cups grated sharp Cheddar cheese
2 cups chopped onion

In a large bowl, sift together:

2 cups all-purpose flour
1½ cups dark rye flour
2 tablespoons baking powder
1/2 teaspoon baking soda

Add:

1/2 cup caraway seeds

Combine the two mixtures just enough to blend. Spoon the batter into the prepared pan. Bake for 20 minutes. Remove the muffins from the pan, and cool on a wire rack. Serve warm.

Variation

Swiss Cheese and Rye

Substitute 4 cups grated Swiss cheese for the Cheddar cheese, and 2 tablespoons spicy-hot prepared mustard for the Worcestershire sauce.

Caraway Cheese Muffins

Offer these light muffins with strawberry jam.

Yield: 12 large muffins   Preheat the oven to 375°F and prepare the pan.

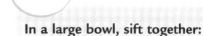

In a large bowl, blend well:
5 large eggs
½ cup butter, melted and cooled
1 cup honey
1 tablespoon vanilla extract
2 tablespoons grated orange peel

Add:
2½ cups low-fat cottage cheese

In a large bowl, sift together:
3½ cups all-purpose flour
4 teaspoons baking powder
1 tablespoon baking soda

Add:
½ cup caraway seeds

Combine the two mixtures just enough to blend. Spoon the batter into the prepared pan. Bake for 20 to 25 minutes. Remove the muffins from the pan, and cool on a wire rack. Serve warm.

Variation

Poppy Seed–Cottage Cheese
Substitute ½ cup poppy seeds for the caraway seeds.

Cheddar Muffins

These muffins are irresistible served with a thick robust soup, grilled sausages, or smoked ham.

Yield: 12 large muffins   Preheat the oven to 425°F and prepare the pan.

In a large bowl, blend well:
2 large eggs
1 cup pure maple syrup*
½ cup butter, melted and cooled
1 cup buttermilk

Add:
4 cups grated sharp Cheddar cheese

*If you'd rather not use maple syrup, just substitute 1 cup buttermilk.

In a large bowl, sift together:
3½ cups all-purpose flour
2 tablespoons baking powder
½ teaspoon baking soda

Combine the two mixtures just enough to blend. Spoon the batter into the prepared pan. Bake for 20 minutes. Remove the muffins from the pan, and cool on a wire rack. Serve warm.

Variation

Bacon Cheddar
Substitute an additional 1 cup buttermilk for the maple syrup. Add 2 tablespoons Dijon mustard, 1 cup finely chopped scallions, and 1 pound lean bacon (crisp-cooked, drained, and crumbled) to the wet ingredients. Add 1 tablespoon ground black pepper to the dry ingredients. Substitute ½ cup snipped fresh dill for the scallions (optional).

More variations of . . . Cheddar Muffins

Apple Cheddar
Substitute 2 cups grated apple for 2 cups Cheddar cheese. Add 1 tablespoon cinnamon, and ½ teaspoon *each* allspice and nutmeg to the dry ingredients. Add ½ cup raisins and 1 cup chopped walnuts to the dry ingredients (optional).

Date Cheese
Add 1 cup cut-up pitted dates and 1 cup chopped walnuts to the dry ingredients.

Sour Cream–Cheddar
Substitute 1 cup sour cream for the buttermilk. Add 1 cup slivered almonds to the dry ingredients.

Cheddar Nut Muffins

These light, tender muffins are absolutely addicting.

Yield: 10 large muffins   Preheat the oven to 400°F and prepare the pan.

In a medium bowl, blend well:
4 large eggs
1 (12-oz.) can lager beer,
    at room temperature

Add:
2 cups grated sharp Cheddar cheese

Topping:
Extra grated Cheddar cheese
Sesame seeds

In a large bowl, blend together:
3½ cups buttermilk baking mix
    (like Bisquick)
1 teaspoon dry mustard

Add:
2 cups chopped pecans or walnuts

Combine the two mixtures just enough to blend. Spoon the batter into the prepared pan. Sprinkle the tops with the extra cheese and sesame seeds. Bake for 18 to 20 minutes. Remove the muffins from the pan, and cool on a wire rack. Serve warm.

Coconut Banana–Swiss Cheese Muffins

These are a delicious choice for a brunch menu.

Yield: 12 large muffins   Preheat the oven to 375°F and prepare the pan.

In a medium bowl, cream well:

½ cup butter, softened

¾ cup sugar

Blend in:

3 large eggs

1 cup milk

1 tablespoon vanilla extract

Add:

2 cups shredded coconut

2 cups mashed very ripe bananas

2 cups grated Swiss cheese

In a large bowl, sift together:

3 cups all-purpose flour

1 tablespoon baking powder

1 teaspoon baking soda

Combine the two mixtures just enough to blend. Spoon the batter into the prepared pan. Bake for 25 to 30 minutes. Remove the muffins from the pan, and cool on a wire rack. Serve warm.

Cottage Cheese–Dill Muffins

Try these savory muffins with rosemary scented roast lamb.

Yield: 12 large muffins

Preheat the oven to 425°F and prepare the pan.

In a large bowl, blend well:
5 large eggs
½ cup butter, melted and cooled
1 cup buttermilk
1 tablespoon Worcestershire sauce

Add:
2½ cups low-fat cottage cheese
1 cup snipped fresh dill
1 cup chopped scallions

In a large bowl, sift together:
3½ cups all-purpose flour
2 tablespoons baking powder
1/2 teaspoon baking soda

Add:
¼ cup caraway seeds (optional)

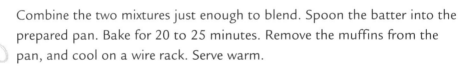

Combine the two mixtures just enough to blend. Spoon the batter into the prepared pan. Bake for 20 to 25 minutes. Remove the muffins from the pan, and cool on a wire rack. Serve warm.

Variation

Potato Cheese
Omit the Worcestershire sauce and caraway seeds. Substitute 1 cup mashed baked potato (not instant) and ¾ cup crumbled feta cheese for 1¾ cups cottage cheese.

Cream Cheese–Herb Muffins

This delicious muffin, fragrant with garlic and herbs, accents grilled or roasted chicken beautifully.

Yield: 12 large muffins   Preheat the oven to 400°F and prepare the pan.

In a large bowl, cream well:
½ cup butter, softened
1 (8-oz.) package cream cheese, softened

Blend in:
5 large eggs
1½ cups milk
4 large garlic cloves, minced
½ cup minced fresh parsley
1½ teaspoons *each* dried oregano, thyme, marjoram, basil, and dill
1 tablespoon ground black pepper
1 cup chopped fresh chives

In a large bowl, sift together:
3½ cups all-purpose flour
2 tablespoons baking powder
1/2 teaspoon baking soda

 Combine the two mixtures just enough to blend. Spoon the batter into the prepared pan. Bake for 20 to 22 minutes. Remove the muffins from the pan, and cool on a wire rack. Serve warm.

Macaroni-and-Cheese Muffins

Who could resist this favorite, brimming with smooth, creamy cheese?

Yield: 12 large muffins   Preheat the oven to 350°F and prepare the pan.

In a large bowl, blend well:
5 cups slightly undercooked
   elbow macaroni
2 large eggs, lightly beaten
1 cup milk
1 teaspoon dry mustard
1 teaspoon cayenne pepper
4 cups grated sharp
   Cheddar cheese*
1 pound lean bacon (cooked,
   drained, and crumbled)
½ cup chopped chives

Spoon into the prepared pan. Bake for 20 minutes, or until the tops are golden. Wait a minute or two before removing the muffins from the pan, then carefully loosen the edges with a spoon or fork, and turn them onto a warm plate. Serve hot.

*Fontina, Gruyère, Jarlsberg, mozzarella, Monterey Jack, and Muenster are equally delicious.

Molasses Cheddar Muffins

These muffins are made for thick, creamy chowders and savory stews.

Yield: 12 large muffins   Preheat the oven to 400°F and prepare the pan.

In a large bowl, blend well:
2 large eggs
1 cup milk
1 cup molasses
1/2 cup butter, melted and cooled

Add:
4 cups grated sharp Cheddar cheese

In a large bowl, sift together:
3 cups all-purpose flour
2 tablespoons baking soda
2 teaspoons cinnamon
1/2 teaspoon *each* nutmeg, ginger,
    and allspice

Combine the two mixtures just enough to blend. Spoon the batter into the prepared pan. Bake for 20 minutes. Remove the muffins from the pan, and cool on a wire rack. Serve warm.

Olive Cheddar Muffins

These savory cheese muffins are just made to accompany steaming bowls of soup.

Yield: 12 large muffins   Preheat the oven to 400°F and prepare the pan.

In a medium bowl, blend well:
3 large eggs
½ cup butter, melted and cooled
1 tablespoon Worcestershire sauce
2 cups buttermilk

Add:
2 cups grated sharp Cheddar cheese
2 (6-oz.) cans pitted black olives,
    drained and chopped

In a large bowl, sift together:
3½ cups all-purpose flour
2 tablespoons baking powder
1 teaspoon baking soda
1/2 teaspoon cayenne pepper

Combine the two mixtures just enough to blend. Spoon the batter into the prepared pan. Bake for 20 minutes. Remove the muffins from the pan, and cool on a wire rack. Serve warm.

Variation

Cheddar Chive
Add 1 cup chopped fresh chives to the wet ingredients.

Parmesan Muffins

Flavored with the pungency of Parmesan cheese and sweet onions, these muffins go well with grilled chicken or lamb.

Yield: 12 large muffins   Preheat the oven to 425°F and prepare the pan.

In a large bowl, blend well:
4 large eggs
½ cup butter, melted and cooled
2 cups plain yogurt

Add:
2 cups finely chopped onion
1 cup minced fresh parsley

In a large bowl, sift together:
3½ cups all-purpose flour
2 tablespoons baking powder
½ teaspoon baking soda
1 cup freshly grated Parmesan cheese
1 tablespoon ground black pepper

Combine the two mixtures just enough to blend. Spoon the batter into the prepared pan. Bake for 20 minutes. Remove the muffins from the pan, and cool on a wire rack. Serve warm.

Variations

Zucchini Parmesan
Substitute 1 cup grated unpeeled zucchini for 1 cup onion.

Cheese Herb
Substitute 2 cups ricotta cheese for the yogurt. Add 1 teaspoon *each* dried rosemary, oregano, and basil to the dry ingredients.

Pear Cheese Muffins

Taking its name from Colby, Wisconsin, Colby is one of the most popular cheeses in the United States. It highlights these fruit-rich, nutty muffins.

Yield: 12 large muffins   Preheat the oven to 400°F and prepare the pan.

In a medium bowl, cream well:
½ cup sugar
½ cup butter, softened

Blend in:
4 large eggs
1 cup heavy cream or buttermilk
1 cup mashed very ripe pears

Add:
2 cups shredded Colby cheese

In a large bowl, sift together:
3 cups all-purpose flour
1 tablespoon baking powder
1 teaspoon baking soda
4 teaspoons cinnamon
1 teaspoon ginger
½ teaspoon *each* allspice, nutmeg, and cloves

Add:
2 cups chopped toasted pecans
1 cup cut-up dried pears

 Combine the two mixtures just enough to blend. Spoon the batter into the prepared pan. Bake for 18 to 20 minutes. Remove the muffins from the pan, and cool on a wire rack. Serve warm.

Poppy Seed–Cheese Muffins

Match these with a soup, salad, or main dish, or with scrambled eggs for breakfast.

Yield: 12 large muffins   Preheat the oven to 400°F and prepare the pan.

In a medium bowl, blend well:
4 large eggs
½ cup butter, melted and cooled
2 cups buttermilk

Add:
1 cup finely chopped scallions
2 cups grated Jarlsberg cheese

In a large bowl, sift together:
3½ cups all-purpose flour
2 tablespoons baking powder
1 teaspoon baking soda

Add:
½ cup poppy seeds

Combine the two mixtures just enough to blend. Spoon the batter into the prepared pan. Bake for 18 to 20 minutes. Remove the muffins from the pan, and cool on a wire rack. Serve warm.

Smoked Cheese and Scallion Muffins

Try these warm with crisp apples, smoked ham, or sausage.

Yield: 12 large muffins   Preheat the oven to 425°F and prepare the pan.

In a medium bowl, blend well:
4 large eggs
2 cups milk
½ cup butter, melted and cooled

Add:
2 cups finely chopped scallions
3 cups grated smoked cheese
    (provolone, Gouda, or mozzarella)
2 teaspoons dried marjoram

In a large bowl, sift together:
3½ cups all-purpose flour
2 tablespoons baking powder
½ teaspoon baking soda
1 tablespoon ground black pepper

Combine the two mixtures just enough to blend. Spoon the batter into the prepared pan. Bake for 20 minutes. Remove the muffins from the pan, and cool on a wire rack. Serve warm.

Spinach Feta Muffins

Freeze any leftovers for grown-up lunchbox treats or to pack along on a picnic.

Yield: 12 to 14 large muffins   Preheat the oven to 425°F and prepare the pan.

In a large bowl, blend well:
3 large eggs
½ cup butter, melted and cooled

Add:
1 cup low-fat cottage cheese
1 cup chopped scallions
2 cloves garlic, minced (optional)
1 cup finely chopped celery
2 (10-oz.) packages frozen chopped
   spinach, thawed and drained well
2 cups crumbled feta cheese
½ cup snipped fresh dill or parsley

In a large bowl, sift together:
3 cups all-purpose flour
2 tablespoons baking soda
1 teaspoon baking powder
1 tablespoon ground black pepper

Combine the two mixtures just enough to blend. Spoon the batter into the prepared pan.

Bake for 20 to 22 minutes. Remove the muffins from the pan, and cool on a wire rack. Serve warm.

Variations

Cheddar and Blue Cheese
Substitute 1 cup *each* grated sharp
Cheddar and crumbled blue cheese for the
feta cheese.

Spinach Sausage
Substitute 1 pound sausage (casings
removed, browned, drained, and crumbled) for the feta cheese.

Three-Cheese Muffins

These are sure to satisfy anyone's hankering for cheese.

Yield: 12 large muffins   Preheat the oven to 425°F and prepare the pan.

In a large bowl, blend well:
3 large eggs
½ cup butter, melted and cooled
2½ cups buttermilk

Add:
2 cups grated Muenster cheese
1 cup *each* grated Swiss
   and mozzarella cheese
2 cups chopped onion

In a large bowl, sift together:
3½ cups all-purpose flour
2 tablespoons baking soda
1 teaspoon baking powder

Combine the two mixtures just enough to blend. Spoon the batter into the prepared pan. Bake for 20 minutes. Remove the muffins from the pan, and cool on a wire rack. Serve warm.

Variation

Jalapeño Cheese
Drain 1 (4.5-oz.) can chopped green chilies and add to the wet ingredients. Substitute 4 cups grated Monterey Jack cheese for the three cheeses.

Tuna Cheese Muffins

There's nothing quite like these muffins for a quick, simple meal.

Yield: 12 to 13 large muffins

Preheat the oven to 425°F and prepare the pan.

In a large bowl, blend well:
3 large eggs
½ cup butter, melted and cooled
2 cups milk

Add:
1 red onion, minced
1 (10-oz.) package frozen chopped
   spinach, thawed and drained well
1 cup grated Swiss cheese
1 cup grated Cheddar cheese
1 (6½-oz.) can chunk tuna
   in water, drained

In a large bowl, sift together:
3½ cups all-purpose flour
2 tablespoons baking powder
½ teaspoon baking soda
2 teaspoons dry mustard
1 teaspoon ground black pepper
½ teaspoon *each* nutmeg and ginger

Add:
1 cup chopped unsalted roasted
   cashews

Combine the two mixtures just enough to blend. Spoon the batter into the prepared pan. Bake for 20 to 22 minutes. Remove the muffins from the pan, and cool on a wire rack. Serve warm.

Chapter 9

Dessert Muffins

For a sweet ending to a busy day or a welcoming treat for unexpected company, try one of these lush, down-home-style dessert muffins. Among the most adaptable desserts, they can be created as stunning centerpieces for special occasions, or as the simple goodies that serve so well for everyday snacks. Choose from the unlimited selections of custards, puddings, dessert sauces, and condiments available to accompany these small, sweet wonders we can't resist!

Apricot Pecan Muffins

Very light and moist, these muffins are great served with sweet creamy butter and peach preserves.

Yield: 12 large muffins   Preheat the oven to 375°F and prepare the pan.

In a medium bowl, blend well:
2 large eggs
½ cup butter, melted and cooled
1 cup milk or sour cream
1 tablespoon vanilla extract
1 cup apricot preserves
3 tablespoons grated lemon
   or orange peel

In a large bowl, sift together:
3 cups all-purpose flour
1 cup sugar
1 tablespoon baking powder
1 teaspoon baking soda
2 tablespoons cinnamon
2 teaspoons nutmeg
1½ teaspoons ginger

Add:
2 cups chopped toasted pecans

Combine the two mixtures just enough to blend. Spoon the batter into the prepared pan. Bake for 18 to 20 minutes. Remove the muffins from the pan, and cool on a wire rack. Serve warm.

Variation

Malted Maple Pecan
Substitute 1 cup pure maple syrup for the apricot preserves. Substitute 1½ cups barley flour for 1½ cups all-purpose flour. Omit the sugar. Add 1 cup malted-milk powder to the dry ingredients.

Banana–Peanut Butter Muffins

These muffins blend two great flavors to make a great after-school snack. They're delicious with tall glasses of cold milk.

Yield: 12 large muffins   Preheat the oven to 375°F and prepare the pan.

In a medium bowl, cream well:
½ cup butter, softened
2 cups peanut butter

Blend in:
4 large eggs
¾ cup honey
1 tablespoon vanilla extract

Add:
2 cups mashed very ripe bananas

In a large bowl, sift together:
3½ cups all-purpose flour
1 tablespoon baking soda
1 tablespoon baking powder
1 tablespoon cinnamon

Add:
2 cups chopped unsalted
    roasted peanuts

Combine the two mixtures just enough to blend. Spoon the batter into the prepared pan. Bake for 20 to 22 minutes. Remove the muffins from the pan, and cool on a wire rack. Serve warm.

Variation

Banana Peanut-Butter Chip
Add 2 cups mini–chocolate chips to the dry ingredients. Omit the peanuts.

Banana Rum-Raisin Muffins

Spiked with a generous amount of rum, these muffins are wonderful with tall mugs of cappuccino.

Yield: 12 large muffins   Preheat the oven to 400°F and prepare the pan.

Soak overnight: 1 cup dark raisins
　　　　　　　　　1 cup rum
　　　　　　　　　Drain and reserve the rum. Set aside.

In a medium bowl, cream well:
1 cup butter, softened
1 cup packed brown sugar

Blend in:
4 large eggs
1 tablespoon vanilla extract

Add:
2 cups mashed very ripe bananas
1 (7-oz.) package coconut

In a large bowl, sift together:
3 cups all-purpose flour
1 tablespoon baking soda
1 tablespoon baking powder
1 tablespoon nutmeg
1 tablespoon cinnamon

Add:
Rum-soaked raisins
1 cup chopped walnuts or pecans

Combine the two mixtures just enough to blend. Spoon the batter into the prepared pan. Bake for 25 minutes. Before removing the muffins from the pan, and while they are still hot, pour 1 tablespoon of the reserved rum over their tops. Allow the rum to soak through, then transfer them onto a wire rack. Serve warm.

Variation

Chocolate Banana Rum
Sift together with the flour, ½ to ¾ cup unsweetened cocoa powder.

Black Magic Muffins

These muffins are deep, dark, and decadent.

Yield: 12 large muffins

Preheat the oven to 400°F and prepare the pan.

In a medium bowl, blend well:
5 large eggs
½ cup butter, melted and cooled
1 tablespoon vanilla extract
1 cup unsweetened cocoa powder
½ cup strong brewed coffee
1 cup buttermilk or sour cream

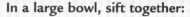

In a large bowl, sift together:
3 cups all-purpose flour
2 teaspoons baking powder
4½ teaspoons baking soda
2 cups sugar

Combine the two mixtures just enough to blend. Spoon the batter into the prepared pan. Bake for 20 minutes. Remove the muffins from the pan, and cool on a wire rack. Serve warm.

Variations

Chocolate Macadamia
Add 2 cups chopped macadamia nuts to the dry ingredients.

Apricot Chocolate
Spoon half the batter into the prepared pan. Top with 1 heaping tablespoon apricot jam, and then with the remaining batter. Bake as directed.

Blackberry Jam Muffins

These are an ideal choice when you're simply in the mood for something sweet.

Yield: 12 large muffins   Preheat the oven to 400°F and prepare the pan.

In a medium bowl, blend well:

4 large eggs

½ cup butter, melted and cooled

1 cup buttermilk

¼ cup bourbon

1 tablespoon grated orange peel

¼ cup unsweetened cocoa powder

Add:

2 cups blackberry
  or black raspberry jam*

*A delicious substitute for 2 cups blackberry or raspberry jam is 2 cups commercial or home-made fig preserves. If you use fig preserves, adding the raisins is optional.

In a large bowl, sift together:

3 cups all-purpose flour

1 cup sugar

2 tablespoons baking powder

1 teaspoon baking soda

1 teaspoon *each* cinnamon, nutmeg,
  and allspice

Add:

2 cups chopped pecans
  or black walnuts**

1 cup raisins

**Black walnuts may be purchased year-round by mail order from Sunnyland Farms and Missouri Dandy Pantry. See Appendix 2 for the addresses and phone numbers.

Combine the two mixtures just enough to blend. Spoon the batter into the prepared pan. Bake for 20 minutes. Remove the muffins from the pan, and cool on a wire rack. Serve warm.

Buttermilk Pecan Muffins

These muffins make a splendid dessert when served with fresh raspberries and fresh summer peaches.

Yield: 12 large muffins　　　　　Preheat the oven to 400°F and prepare the pan.

In a medium bowl, blend well:
5 large eggs
½ cup butter, melted and cooled
1½ cups buttermilk
1 tablespoon vanilla extract

In a large bowl, sift together:
3 cups all-purpose flour
2 tablespoons baking soda
2 teaspoons cinnamon
½ teaspoon *each* cloves, ginger, and nutmeg
1 cup packed brown sugar

Add:
2 cups chopped pecans

Combine the two mixtures just enough to blend. Spoon the batter into the prepared pan. Bake for 20 minutes. Remove the muffins from the pan, and cool on a wire rack. Serve warm.

Variation

Pecan Orange
Substitute ¾ cup fresh orange juice for ¾ cup buttermilk.

Carob Walnut Muffins

With a flavor all its own, carob blends perfectly in these luscious, fudgy treats. Enjoy them with a cold glass of milk.

Yield: 12 large muffins   Preheat the oven to 400°F and prepare the pan.

In a medium bowl, blend well:
4 large eggs
½ cup butter, melted and cooled
1 tablespoon vanilla extract
1½ cups buttermilk
¾ cup carob powder
½ cup fresh orange juice
1 tablespoon grated orange peel

In a large bowl, sift together:
3 cups all-purpose flour
2 tablespoons baking powder
1 teaspoon baking soda
1 cup sugar
1 tablespoon nutmeg

Add:
2 cups chopped walnuts or pecans

Combine the two mixtures just enough to blend. Spoon the batter into the prepared pan. Bake for 18 to 20 minutes. Remove the muffins from the pan, and cool on a wire rack. Serve warm.

Chocolate Amaretto Crunch Muffins

Amaretto liqueur contributes its silky almond flavor to these fabulous muffins.

Yield: 12 large muffins   Preheat the oven to 400°F and prepare the pan.

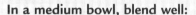

In a medium bowl, blend well:
5 large eggs
½ cup butter, melted and cooled
1 cup sour cream
2 teaspoons vanilla extract
½ cup Amaretto liqueur

In a large bowl, sift together:
3 cups all-purpose flour
1 cup packed brown sugar
2 tablespoons baking powder
½ teaspoon baking soda

Add:
2 cups slivered almonds, toasted
   and cooled
1 cup mini–chocolate chips

Additional ingredient:
Amaretto liqueur

Combine the two mixtures just enough to blend. Spoon the batter into the prepared pan. Bake for 20 minutes. Before removing the muffins from the pan, while they are still hot from the oven, pour 1 tablespoon Amaretto over the tops. Allow the Amaretto to soak through, and transfer onto a wire rack. Serve warm.

Variation

Hazelnut Crunch
Substitute ½ cup hazelnut liqueur for the Amaretto, and 2 cups chopped toasted hazelnuts for the almonds. Bake as directed. Before removing the muffins from the pan, while they are still hot from the oven, pour 1 tablespoon hazelnut liqueur over the tops. Allow the liqueur to soak through, and transfer onto a wire rack. Serve warm.

Chocolate Chip–Pistachio Muffins

These delectable muffins will satisfy any sweet tooth.

Yield: 12 large muffins   Preheat the oven to 375°F and prepare the pan.

In a medium bowl, blend well:
2 large eggs
½ cup butter, melted and cooled
2 teaspoons vanilla extract
2 cups heavy cream
1 tablespoon grated lemon peel

In a large bowl, sift together:
3 cups all-purpose flour
1 cup sugar
1 tablespoon baking powder
½ teaspoon baking soda
1 teaspoon cinnamon

Add:
2 cups mini-chocolate chips
1 cup chopped unsalted pistachio
    nuts

Filling:
¾ cup raspberry jam, or other fruit jam

Combine the two mixtures just enough to blend. Spoon half the batter into the prepared pan. Top with 1 tablespoon raspberry jam, and then with the remaining batter. Bake for 20 to 25 minutes. Remove the muffins from the pan, and cool on a wire rack. Serve warm.

Chocolate-Coconut Pecan Muffins

These muffins are just plain fabulous.

Yield: 12 large muffins   Preheat the oven to 400°F and prepare the pan.

In a small saucepan, stir until melted:
1 (4-oz.) bar sweet baking chocolate, in pieces
½ cup boiling water

In a medium bowl, blend well:
4 large eggs
½ cup butter, melted and cooled
1 tablespoon vanilla extract
1 cup sour cream
1 tablespoon instant coffee powder

Add:
Chocolate mixture, cooled

In a large bowl, sift together:
3½ cups all-purpose flour
2 tablespoons baking powder
½ teaspoon baking soda
1 tablespoon cinnamon
1½ cups sugar

Add:
1 (7-oz.) package coconut
2 cups chopped pecans

Combine the two mixtures just enough to blend. Spoon the batter into the prepared pan. Bake for 20 to 22 minutes. Remove the muffins from the pan, and cool on a wire rack. Serve warm.

Variation

Chocolate-Coconut Rum
Before removing the muffins from the pan, while they are still hot from the oven, pour 1 tablespoon light rum over the tops. Allow the rum to soak through, and then transfer them onto a wire rack. Serve warm.

Chocolate Marble Muffins

Mmmmmmmmmmmm . . .

Yield: 12 large muffins

Preheat the oven to 400°F and prepare the pan.

In a medium bowl, blend well:
4 large eggs
½ cup butter, melted and cooled
2 cups sour cream
1 tablespoon vanilla extract
1 teaspoon almond extract

Additional ingredient:
¾ cup chocolate syrup

In a large bowl, sift together:
4 cups all-purpose flour
1½ cups sugar
2 tablespoons baking powder
1 teaspoon baking soda
2 teaspoons cinnamon

Combine the two mixtures just enough to blend. Spoon half the batter into the prepared pan. Top with 1 tablespoon chocolate syrup, then cover with the remaining batter. Using a toothpick, swirl the chocolate to marbleize. Bake for 20 minutes. Remove the muffins from the pan, and cool on a wire rack. Serve warm.

Chocolate Mayonnaise Muffins

When only chocolate will do, this indulgence is not to be missed.

Yield: 12 large muffins

Preheat the oven to 400°F and prepare the pan.

In a small bowl, mix until smooth:
1 cup unsweetened cocoa powder
1 cup boiling water

In a medium bowl, blend well:
3 large eggs
1½ cups real mayonnaise
1 tablespoon vanilla extract

Add:
Cocoa mixture, cooled

In a large bowl, sift together:
3½ cups all-purpose flour
2 cups sugar
2 tablespoons baking powder
½ teaspoon baking soda

Add:
2 cups mini-chocolate chips

Combine the two mixtures just enough to blend. Spoon the batter into the prepared pan.

Bake for 18 to 20 minutes. Remove the muffins from the pan, and cool on a wire rack. Serve warm.

Variations

Chocolate Mint
Substitute 1 tablespoon mint/peppermint or wintergreen extract for the vanilla and 2 cups mint-flavored chocolate chips for the minichips.

Marbled Chocolate Cheesecake
To prepare the filling, blend 4 oz. softened cream cheese, 1 egg, ¼ cup sugar, and 2 teaspoons vanilla extract. Make the filling before you start the batter so that the muffins will be ready to go into the oven promptly.

Spoon half the batter into the prepared pan. Divide the filling evenly over the batter. Cover with the remaining batter. Bake as directed.

Cinnamon Almond Muffins

These luscious, aromatic muffins are speckled with crunchy slivered almonds.

Yield: 12 large muffins   Preheat the oven to 400°F and prepare the pan.

For Cinnamon Butter, stir together:
4 tablespoons butter, melted
2 tablespoons cinnamon

In a medium bowl, blend well:
5 large eggs
½ cup butter, melted and cooled
2 cups sour cream
1 tablespoon almond extract

In a large bowl, sift together:
3 cups all-purpose flour
1 cup sugar
2 tablespoons baking powder
1 teaspoon baking soda
1 tablespoon cinnamon

Add:
2 cups slivered almonds, toasted

Combine the two mixtures just enough to blend. Spoon the batter into the prepared pan. Bake for 18 to 20 minutes. Brush the tops with the Cinnamon Butter while the muffins are still hot from the oven. Remove the muffins from the pan, and cool on a wire rack. Serve warm.

Variation

Raspberry Almond
Prepare Cinnamon Almond Muffins as directed. Spoon half the batter into the pan. Top with 1 tablespoon raspberry preserves, then cover with the remaining batter and bake as directed.

Cocoa Applesauce Muffins

This sweet muffin is perfect to serve with tall glasses of ice-cold lemonade.

Yield: 12 large muffins   Preheat the oven to 400°F and prepare the pan.

In a medium bowl, cream well:
1½ cups sugar
½ cup butter, softened

Blend in:
4 large eggs
1 tablespoon vanilla extract
2 cups unsweetened applesauce

In a large bowl, sift together:
3 cups all-purpose flour
1 tablespoon baking powder
1 teaspoon baking soda
½ cup unsweetened cocoa powder
1 tablespoon cinnamon

Add:
1 cup chopped walnuts
1 cup raisins

Combine the two mixtures just enough to blend. Spoon the batter into the prepared pan. Bake for 18 to 20 minutes. Remove the muffins from the pan, and cool on a wire rack. Serve warm.

Coconut Muffins

These velvety light coconut macaroon muffins will make your mouth water.

Yield: 12 large muffins

Preheat the oven to 400°F and prepare the pan.

In a medium bowl, blend well:
5 large eggs
½ cup butter, melted and cooled
2 cups sour cream
1 tablespoon coconut
  or vanilla extract

Add:
1 (7-oz.) package coconut

In a large bowl, sift together:
3 cups all-purpose flour
1½ cups sugar
2 tablespoons baking powder
1 teaspoon baking soda

Combine the two mixtures just enough to blend. Spoon the batter into the prepared pan. Bake for 18 to 20 minutes. Remove the muffins from the pan, and cool on a wire rack. Serve warm.

Variations

Chocolate Chip–Coconut
Add 2 cups mini–chocolate chips to the dry ingredients.

Coconut Date
Add 1 cup cut-up pitted dates to the dry ingredients.

Coffee Walnut Muffins

Serve these with cream cheese and fresh raspberries.

Yield: 12 large muffins   Preheat the oven to 400°F and prepare the pan.

In a medium bowl, blend well:
4 large eggs
½ cup butter, melted and cooled
1 tablespoon vanilla extract
1½ cups milk
⅓ cup instant espresso
   or coffee powder

In a large bowl, sift together:
3 cups all-purpose flour
2 tablespoons baking powder
½ teaspoon baking soda
1 cup sugar

Add:
2 cups chopped walnuts
1 cup mini–chocolate chips

Combine the two mixtures just enough to blend. Spoon the batter into the prepared pan. Bake for 20 to 25 minutes. Remove the muffins from the pan, and cool on a wire rack. Serve warm.

Variations

Amaretto Walnut
Omit the coffee powder and chocolate chips. Substitute 1 tablespoon almond extract for the vanilla and ½ cup Amaretto liqueur for the milk. Add 1 tablespoon grated orange peel to the wet ingredients. Bake as directed.

Prepare the glaze. In a saucepan over medium heat, blend 10 oz. orange marmalade, 5 oz. apricot preserves, and ¼ cup Amaretto liqueur until melted. Before removing the muffins from the pan, while they are still hot, drizzle 1 tablespoon glaze over the tops. (Refrigerate any leftover glaze to use as a spread.) Top with slivered almonds. Transfer the muffins onto a wire rack. Serve warm.

Coffee and Cream
Substitute ½ cup Kahlua or other coffee-flavored liqueur for the milk. Omit the chocolate chips.

Prepare the filling. In a small bowl, blend 3 oz. cream cheese, softened, and ⅓ cup powdered sugar until smooth. Spoon half the batter into the prepared pan. Top with 1 tablespoon cream cheese filling. Cover with the remaining batter. Bake as directed.

Gingerbread Muffins

Always a favorite, these are delicious crowned with fresh applesauce, brandied fruit, or a scoop of vanilla ice cream. They're equally tasty with hot or cold curried salads.

Yield: 11 large muffins   Preheat the oven to 375°F and prepare the pan.

In a medium bowl, blend well:
3 large eggs
1 cup molasses
½ cup butter, melted and cooled
1 cup buttermilk
1 tablespoon grated orange peel
1 tablespoon vanilla extract
2 tablespoons instant coffee granules

In a large bowl, sift together:
3¼ cups all-purpose flour
1 cup packed brown sugar
2 tablespoons baking soda
2 teaspoons ginger
2 teaspoons cinnamon
½ teaspoon cloves
1 teaspoon nutmeg

Add:
1 cup chopped pecans or currants
(optional)

Combine the two mixtures just enough to blend. Spoon the batter into the prepared pan. Bake for 18 to 20 minutes. Remove the muffins from the pan, and cool on a wire rack. Serve warm.

Variations

Sour Cream–Gingerbread
Substitute 1 cup sour cream for the buttermilk.

Pumpkin Gingerbread
Substitute 1 cup mashed fresh or canned solid-pack pumpkin for the buttermilk.

Orange Gingerbread
Substitute 1 cup fresh orange juice for the buttermilk.

Hazelnut Fig Muffins

Delicious served warm with ice cream or with black cherry preserves, these muffins can also be paired with thin slices of prosciutto.

Yield: 12 large muffins

Preheat the oven to 400°F and prepare the pan.

In a medium bowl, blend well:
4 large eggs
½ cup butter, melted and cooled
1 cup milk
1 tablespoon vanilla extract
1 tablespoon grated orange peel
2 tablespoons unsweetened
   cocoa powder
½ cup Madeira or sherry

In a large bowl, sift together:
2 cups all-purpose flour
1 cup whole-wheat flour
1 cup packed brown sugar
4 teaspoons baking soda
2 teaspoons baking powder
1 tablespoon cinnamon
1 teaspoon nutmeg
¼ teaspoon cloves

Add:
2 cups cut-up Calimyrna
   or Black Mission dried figs
2 cups chopped toasted hazelnuts
   or pecans

Combine the two mixtures just enough to blend. Spoon the batter into the prepared pan. Bake for 18 to 20 minutes. Remove the muffins from the pan, and cool on a wire rack. Serve warm.

Honey Lemon Muffins

Absolutely delicious served with sugared strawberries or raspberries.

Yield: 12 large muffins   Preheat the oven to 375°F and prepare the pan.

In a medium bowl, blend well:
5 large eggs
1 cup honey
½ cup butter, melted and cooled
¾ cup fresh lemon juice
1 tablespoon lemon or vanilla extract
2 tablespoons grated lemon peel

Add:
½ cup peeled, grated fresh ginger
   (optional)

In a large bowl, sift together:
3¼ cups all-purpose flour
2 tablespoons baking powder
½ teaspoon baking soda
1 tablespoon cinnamon
¼ teaspoon *each* nutmeg and
   allspice

Combine the two mixtures just enough to blend. Spoon the batter into the prepared pan. Bake for 20 minutes. Remove the muffins from the pan, and cool on a wire rack. Serve warm.

Honey Walnut Muffins

This sweet treat is accented with a honey glaze and a crunchy filling.

Yield: 12 large muffins   Preheat the oven to 400°F and prepare the pan.

In a small bowl, blend filling:
2 cups chopped walnuts
½ cup packed brown sugar
2 tablespoons cinnamon
4 tablespoons butter, melted

In a medium bowl, blend well:
2 large eggs
½ cup butter, melted and cooled
2 cups buttermilk

In a large bowl, sift together:
3 cups all-purpose flour
1 cup sugar
4 teaspoons baking powder
1 teaspoon baking soda

Additional ingredient:
½ cup honey

Combine the two mixtures just enough to blend. Spoon half the batter into the prepared pan. Place 1 tablespoon filling in the center. Cover completely with the remaining batter. Bake for 18 to 20 minutes. Before removing the muffins from the pan, while they are still hot, brush them with honey. Transfer the muffins onto a wire rack. Serve warm.

Ice Cream Muffins

This irresistible recipe makes muffins that are delicate, light, and just as delicious as they sound.

Yield: 12 large muffins   Preheat the oven to 400°F and prepare the pan.

In a large bowl, blend well:
½ gallon ice cream, melted
1 tablespoon vanilla extract

Add:
3½ cups self-rising flour

**Mix the Cinnamon Sugar
in a medium bowl:**
¾ cup granulated sugar
2 tablespoons cinnamon
1 teaspoon nutmeg

Combine this mixture just enough to blend. Spoon the batter into the prepared pan. Top generously with the Cinnamon Sugar. Bake for 20 to 22 minutes. Remove the muffins from the pan, and cool on a wire rack. Serve warm.

Maple Pecan Muffins

Pure maple syrup gives its delicious rich flavor to these muffins. They're perfect at breakfast with ham and eggs.

Yield: 12 large muffins   Preheat the oven to 400°F and prepare the pan.

In a medium bowl, blend well:
5 large eggs
1 cup pure maple syrup
½ cup butter, melted and cooled
1 cup sour cream
1 tablespoon maple or vanilla
   extract

In a large bowl, sift together:
3¼ cups all-purpose flour
¾ cup packed brown sugar
2 tablespoons baking powder
1 teaspoon baking soda
1 tablespoon allspice

Add:
2 cups chopped pecans

Combine the two mixtures just enough to blend. Spoon the batter into the prepared pan. Bake for 20 minutes. Remove the muffins from the pan, and cool on a wire rack. Serve warm.

Variations

Cinnamon Pecan
Substitute 1 tablespoon cinnamon for allspice. In a small bowl, mix ½ cup granulated sugar, 4 teaspoons cinnamon, and ½ teaspoon nutmeg. Before baking, sprinkle the tops of the muffins generously with this cinnamon-sugar topping, keeping any leftover for another use.

Maple Walnut
Substitute 2 cups chopped walnuts for the pecans. Add 1 cup cut-up pitted dates to the dry ingredients.

Mocha Hazelnut Spice Muffins

Try these muffins with fresh raspberries and cream.

Yield: 12 large muffins   Preheat the oven to 400°F and prepare the pan.

In a medium bowl, blend well:
4 large eggs
½ cup butter, melted and cooled
⅓ cup unsweetened cocoa powder
3 tablespoons instant espresso or
   coffee powder
1½ cups buttermilk
2 teaspoons vanilla or maple extract

In a large bowl, sift together:
3 cups all-purpose flour
1½ cups packed brown sugar
1 tablespoon baking powder
1 tablespoon baking soda
1 teaspoon *each* nutmeg, cinnamon,
   and allspice
¼ teaspoon cloves

Add:
2 cups chopped toasted hazelnuts
½ cup poppy seeds

Combine the two mixtures just enough to blend. Spoon the batter into the prepared pan. Bake for 20 minutes. Remove the muffins from the pan, and cool on a wire rack. Serve warm.

Variation

Raspberry Mocha
After blending the batter, fold in 2 cups fresh red raspberries. Bake as directed.

Orange Almond Muffins

These muffins are delicious with fresh peach ice cream.

Yield: 12 large muffins

Preheat the oven to 375°F and prepare the pan.

Combine glaze in a small saucepan:

⅓ cup honey
⅓ cup Amaretto liqueur
⅓ cup fresh orange juice

Over low heat, stir until blended. Remove glaze from heat and set aside.

In a medium bowl, blend well:

2 large eggs
½ cup butter, melted and cooled
1 teaspoon vanilla extract
½ cup honey
½ cup fresh orange juice
½ cup milk
½ cup Amaretto liqueur
1 tablespoon grated orange peel

In a large bowl, sift together:

3 cups all-purpose flour
4 teaspoons baking powder
1 cup sugar

Add:

2 cups slivered almonds

Combine the two mixtures just enough to blend. Spoon the batter into the prepared pan. Bake for 20 minutes. Before removing the muffins from the pan, while they are still hot from the oven, pour 1 tablespoon glaze over the tops. Allow the glaze to soak through, and then transfer onto a wire rack. Serve warm.

Peanut Butter Muffins

These luscious, melt-in-your-mouth treats are a peanut butter lover's dream!

Yield: 12 large muffins

Preheat the oven to 375°F and prepare the pan.

In a medium bowl, cream well:
3 cups smooth peanut butter
1 cup butter, softened
1 cup packed light brown sugar
In a medium bowl, blend well:
3 large eggs
1¾ cups buttermilk
1 tablespoon vanilla extract

In a large bowl, sift together:
3½ cups all-purpose flour
4 teaspoons baking powder
2 teaspoons baking soda
Cut in peanut butter mixture to dry ingredients, blending until mixture resembles coarse meal.

Combine the two mixtures just enough to blend. Spoon the batter into the prepared pan. Bake for 20 to 25 minutes. Remove the muffins from the pan, and cool on a wire rack. Serve warm.

Variation

Peanut Butter–Chocolate Chip
Add 2 cups mini–chocolate chips to the dry ingredients.

Poppy Seed Muffins

With their sweet fragrance and slightly crunchy texture, these muffins are wonderful served with a dollop of raspberry jam.

Yield: 12 large muffins   Preheat the oven to 400°F and prepare the pan.

In a medium bowl, blend well:
5 large eggs
½ cup butter, melted and cooled
2 cups sour cream
1 tablespoon vanilla or lemon extract
2 tablespoons grated lemon peel

In a large bowl, sift together:
3¼ cups all-purpose flour
1 cup sugar
1 tablespoon baking soda
1 tablespoon baking powder

Add:
½ cup poppy seeds

Combine the two mixtures just enough to blend. Spoon the batter into the prepared pan. Bake for 18 to 20 minutes. Remove the muffins from the pan, and cool on a wire rack. Serve warm.

Pound-Cake Muffins

A simple, perfectly textured muffin that you can easily turn into a fabulous dessert.

Yield: 12 large muffins   Preheat the oven to 375°F and prepare the pan.

In a large bowl, cream well:
1½ cups sugar
1 cup butter, softened

Blend in:
4 large eggs
1 tablespoon vanilla extract
2 cups sour cream

In a large bowl, sift together:
3 cups all-purpose flour
1 tablespoon baking powder
½ teaspoon baking soda

Combine the two mixtures just enough to blend. Spoon the batter into the prepared pan. Bake for 20 minutes. Remove the muffins from the pan, and cool on a wire rack. Serve warm.

Variations

Nutmeg
Add 2 tablespoons ground nutmeg, or 1 to 2 freshly grated whole nutmegs, to the dry ingredients.

Apricot Brandy
Substitute 1 teaspoon *each* orange, rum, almond, vanilla, and lemon extracts for the vanilla extract, and ½ cup apricot brandy for ½ cup sour cream.

Chocolate Chip
Add 2 cups mini-chocolate chips to the dry ingredients.

Raisin Tea Muffins

With a spunky flavor from a generous amount of whiskey, these moist, light muffins are best sampled while sitting down! They are delicious with jams and fruit preserves.

Yield: 12 to 13 large muffins   Preheat the oven to 400°F and prepare the pan.

In a large bowl, blend well:
1½ cups golden raisins
1½ cups dried currants
1½ cups packed brown sugar
3 cups strong brewed black tea
  (like Earl Grey)
1 cup whiskey or dry sherry

Other ingredients:
3 large eggs
1 tablespoon vanilla extract
3½ cups self-rising flour
1 tablespoon cinnamon

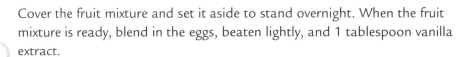

Cover the fruit mixture and set it aside to stand overnight. When the fruit mixture is ready, blend in the eggs, beaten lightly, and 1 tablespoon vanilla extract.

In a large bowl, sift together the flour and the cinnamon. Pour in the fruit mixture and combine just enough to blend. Spoon the batter into the prepared pan. Bake for 20 minutes. Remove the muffins from the pan, and cool on a wire rack. Serve warm.

Raspberry–Chocolate Chip Muffins

These delicious muffins can be served with French vanilla ice cream.

Yield: 12 large muffins   Preheat the oven to 375°F and prepare the pan.

In a medium bowl, cream well:
1 cup butter, softened
1 cup sugar

Blend in:
4 large eggs
1 cup sour cream
1 tablespoon vanilla extract

In a large bowl, sift together:
3 cups all-purpose flour
1 tablespoon baking powder
½ teaspoon baking soda

Add:
2 cups mini–chocolate chips

Additional ingredient:
¾ cup raspberry preserves,
   or any fruit jam

Combine the two mixtures just enough to blend. Spoon half the batter into the prepared pan. Top with 1 tablespoon preserves, and then with the remaining batter.

In a small bowl, mix ½ cup granulated sugar, 4 teaspoons cinnamon, and ½ teaspoon nutmeg. Sprinkle the tops generously with this Cinnamon Sugar, keeping any leftover for another use.

Bake for 20 minutes. Remove the muffins from the pan, and cool on a wire rack. Serve warm.

Rum Raisin Muffins

These muffins have a wonderful taste that is enhanced by a lacing of rum.

Yield: 12 large muffins   Preheat the oven to 400°F and prepare the pan.

Soak overnight: 2 cups dark raisins
                           1 cup rum
                           Drain and reserve the rum. Set aside.

In a medium bowl, cream well:
1 cup butter, softened
1 cup sugar

Blend in:
4 large eggs
2 cups sour cream
1 tablespoon vanilla extract

In a large bowl, sift together:
3 cups all-purpose flour
1 tablespoon baking powder
1 tablespoon baking soda
1 tablespoon nutmeg

Add:
Rum-soaked raisins

Combine the two mixtures just enough to blend. Spoon the batter into the prepared pan. Bake for 20 to 22 minutes.

Before removing the muffins from the pan, while they are hot, pour 1 tablespoon of the reserved rum over the tops. Allow the rum to soak through, and then transfer the muffins onto a wire rack. Serve warm.

Variations

Chocolate Rum Raisin
Add 1 cup chopped walnuts to the dry ingredients. Add ⅓ cup unsweetened cocoa powder and 2 tablespoons instant espresso or coffee powder to the wet ingredients.

Rum Eggnog
Substitute 2 cups eggnog (commercial or home-made) for the sour cream.

Cinnamon Raisin
Substitute 1 tablespoon cinnamon for the nutmeg. Omit the rum in this version. Add 2 cups raisins to the dry ingredients.

Sour Cream—Coffeecake Muffins

These mouthwatering muffins are a very special, simple treat.

Yield: 12 large muffins   Preheat the oven to 400°F and prepare the pan.

Combine filling in a small bowl: ½ cup packed brown sugar

1 cup chopped pecans or walnuts

2 tablespoons all-purpose flour

2 teaspoons cinnamon

1 teaspoon nutmeg

2 tablespoons butter, melted

In a medium bowl, blend well:

4 large eggs

1 cup sour cream or milk

1 tablespoon vanilla extract

2 teaspoons instant coffee powder

In a large bowl, sift together:

3 cups all-purpose flour

1 cup sugar

2 tablespoons baking powder

Cut in:

1 cup butter, softened

Blend until mixture resembles coarse meal.

Combine the two mixtures just enough to blend. Spoon half the batter into the prepared pan. Top with 1 tablespoon reserved brown sugar mixture and then with the remaining batter.

In a small bowl, mix ½ cup granulated sugar, 4 teaspoons cinnamon, and ½ teaspoon nutmeg. Sprinkle the tops generously with this Cinnamon Sugar, keeping any leftover for another use.

Bake for 20 to 25 minutes. Remove the muffins from the pan, and cool on a wire rack. Serve warm.

Spice Muffins

Heavy cream and apple butter gives these muffins a fine, creamy texture and a delicate crumb.

Yield: 12 large muffins   Preheat the oven to 400°F and prepare the pan.

In a medium bowl, cream well:
1 cup sugar
1 cup butter, softened

Blend in:
4 large eggs
1 tablespoon vanilla extract
1 cup heavy cream or buttermilk
1 cup pure apple butter

In a large bowl, sift together:
3 cups all-purpose flour
1 tablespoon baking powder
1 teaspoon baking soda
2 tablespoons unsweetened
  cocoa powder
2 teaspoons nutmeg
1 teaspoon ginger
1 tablespoon cinnamon
1 tablespoon cloves
½ teaspoon allspice

Add:
1 cup raisins
1 (7-oz.) package coconut

Combine the two mixtures just enough to blend. Spoon the batter into the prepared pan. Bake for 18 to 20 minutes. Remove the muffins from the pan, and cool on a wire rack. Serve warm.

Variation

Sour Cream–Raisin
Substitute 2 cups sour cream for the heavy cream and apple butter. Substitute 2 cups chopped walnuts for the coconut.

Spiced Mandarin Orange Muffins

This glorious muffin is laced with a rich, lively taste.

Yield: 14 to 15 large muffins

Preheat the oven to 400°F
and prepare the pan.

In a medium bowl, blend well:
5 large eggs
½ cup butter, melted and cooled
2 cups sour cream
1 tablespoon orange
or vanilla extract

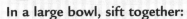

In a large bowl, sift together:
4 cups all-purpose flour
1½ cups sugar
2 tablespoons baking powder
1 teaspoon baking soda
1½ teaspoons *each* nutmeg,
cinnamon, and ground cardamom

Hold aside:
2 (15-oz.) cans mandarin orange
sections, drained

Combine the two mixtures just enough to blend. Fold in the orange
sections. Spoon the batter into the prepared pan. Bake for 20 to 25
minutes. Remove the muffins from the pan, and cool on a wire rack.
Serve warm.

Sweet Plum Muffins

The lush taste of spiced plums beautifully complements vanilla ice cream or a creamy custard.

Yield: 12 large muffins   Preheat the oven to 425°F and prepare the pan.

In a medium bowl, blend well:
4 large eggs
½ cup butter, melted and cooled
½ cup pure maple syrup
1 tablespoon grated orange
   or lemon peel
2 teaspoons vanilla
   or almond extract

Add:
1 (30-oz.) can whole purple plums,
   drained, pitted, and mashed
   (about 1⅔ cups)

In a large bowl, sift together:
3 cups all-purpose flour
2 tablespoons baking powder
½ teaspoon baking soda
1 tablespoon cinnamon
1 teaspoon nutmeg or ginger

Add:
1 cup raisins
1 cup *each* chopped toasted pecans
   and hazelnuts

Combine the two mixtures just enough to blend. Spoon the batter into the prepared pan. Bake for 18 to 20 minutes. Remove the muffins from the pan, and cool on a wire rack. Serve warm.

Sweet Potato–Peach Muffins

These are muffins with true Southern comfort. Sweet potatoes have been grown in the South since before the first settlers arrived in the early seventeenth century. For a simple, fresh dessert, add a dollop of cream or vanilla ice cream to top off their rich flavor.

Yield: 12 large muffins

Preheat the oven to 375°F and prepare the pan.

In a medium bowl, cream well:
1 cup packed brown sugar
1 cup butter, softened

Blend in:
3 large eggs
1 tablespoon vanilla extract
1 tablespoon grated orange peel

Add:
2 cups mashed baked sweet potatoes
1 cup peach preserves

In a large bowl, sift together:
3 cups all-purpose flour
1 tablespoon baking powder
1 tablespoon baking soda
1 teaspoon *each* ginger, nutmeg, allspice, and cinnamon
½ teaspoon cloves

Add:
2 cups chopped pecans

Combine the two mixtures just enough to blend. Spoon the batter into the prepared pan. Bake for 25 minutes. Remove the muffins from the pan, and cool on a wire rack. Serve warm.

Variation

Sweet Potato–Gingerbread
Substitute ¾ cup molasses and ¼ cup milk for the peach preserves.

Walnut–Cream Cheese Muffins

These are delicious with just a dusting of powdered sugar.

Yield: 12 large muffins   Preheat the oven to 375°F and prepare the pan.

In a medium bowl, cream well:
1 (8-oz.) package cream cheese, softened
2 cups sugar

Blend in:
4 large eggs
1 tablespoon vanilla extract
1 cup sour cream

In a large bowl, sift together:
3 cups all-purpose flour
1 tablespoon baking powder

Add:
2 cups chopped walnuts

 Combine the two mixtures just enough to blend. Spoon the batter into the prepared pan. Bake for 20 minutes. Remove the muffins from the pan, and cool on a wire rack. Serve warm.

Variations

Mocha Cheesecake
Add 2 tablespoons instant coffee powder and ¼ cup unsweetened cocoa powder to the wet ingredients, and 1 tablespoon cinnamon to the dry ingredients.

Pumpkin Pecan Cheesecake
Substitute 2 cups packed light brown sugar for the granulated sugar, 1 cup mashed fresh or canned (solid-pack) pumpkin for the sour cream, and 2 cups chopped pecans for the walnuts. Add 1 teaspoon *each* cinnamon and nutmeg, and ½ teaspoon cloves to the dry ingredients.

Date Nut–Cream Cheese
Add 2 cups cut-up pitted dates to the dry ingredients.

Appendix 1

Equivalents and Conversions Tables

Equivalents Table

Equivalents for Common Ingredients

Ingredient	Measure	Weight
Almonds		
Blanched whole	1 cup	6 oz.
Chopped or slivered	1 cup	5 oz.
	3½ cups	1 lb.
Apples		
1 medium, chopped	1 cup	6 oz.
Apricots		
fresh	8 to 10 small	1 lb.
dried, pitted	1 cup packed	8 oz.
preserves	1 cup	12-ounce jar
Bananas		
2 medium, mashed	1 cup	8 oz.
Berries		
1 pint	2 cups	10 oz.
Butter, unsalted "sweet"		
1 stick	8 tablespoons (½ cup)	4 oz.
2 sticks	1 cup	½ lb.
Carrots		
2 medium, peeled, grated	1 cup	4 oz.

Ingredient	Measure	Weight
Cashews	1 cup	6 oz.
Cheese		
Blue	1 cup	2 oz.
Cheddar	1 cup	3 oz.
Feta	1 cup	5 oz.
Gorgonzola	1 cup	2 oz.
Monterey Jack	1 cup	3 oz.
Mozzarella	1 cup	4 oz.
Muenster	1 cup	3 oz.
Parmesan	1 cup	3 oz.
Provolone	1 cup	4 oz.
Swiss or Jarlsberg	1 cup	4 oz.
Cherries		
Candied	1 cup packed	8 oz.
Sour	6 cups	2 lbs.
Chocolate, semisweet or unsweetened	1 square	1 oz.
Chocolate chips	1 cup	6 oz.
Citrus peel, candied	1 cup packed	8 oz.
Cocoa, unsweetened	1 cup	4 oz.

Ingredient	Measure	Weight
Coconut, sweetened, shredded	1 cup	3 oz.
Cornmeal	¾ cup	4 oz.
Currants	1 cup	5 oz.
Dates, pitted and chopped	1 cup	6 oz.
Eggs 4 or 5 whole	1 cup	4 to 5 oz.
Egg whites 4 large	½ cup	4 oz.
8 to 10 large	1 cup	8 oz.
Flour		
All-purpose, sifted	¾ cup	2½ oz.
	4 cups	1 lb.
All-purpose, unsifted	½ cup	2½ oz.
	¾ cup	3½ oz.
	1 cup	5 oz.
Rye	1 cup	5½ oz.
Whole-wheat, unsifted	1 cup	5½ oz.
Hazelnuts, whole	1½ cups	8 oz.

Ingredient	Measure	Weight
Honey	1½ cups	12 oz.
Lemon juice	1 cup	8 oz.
Milk	1 cup	8 oz.
Molasses	1½ cups	12 oz.
Nectarines, fresh 2 medium, sliced	1 cup	4 oz.
Oranges 1 medium	6 to 8 tablespoons juice	4 oz.
Peaches 1 medium 1 large	½ cup 1 cup	4 oz. 6 to 8 oz.
Peanuts, shelled	1 cup	5 oz.
Peanut butter	1 cup	9 oz.
Pears	1 medium	6 oz.
Pecans, **shelled and chopped**	2 tablespoons 1 cup ¾ cup	½ oz. 4 oz. 3 oz.
Pineapple, candied	1 cup packed	8 oz.

Ingredient	Measure	Weight
Plums	4 medium, sliced	1½ cups
Poppy seeds, whole	¾ cup	4 oz.
Prunes, dried, pitted, chopped	1 cup packed	8 oz.
Pumpkin	1 small (3 lbs.)	3 cups purée
Raisins, seedless	1 cup	6 oz.
Rhubarb, fresh, diced	4 cups	1¼ lbs.
Rolled oats	5 cups	1 lb.
Shortening	2 cups	1 lb.
Sugar, brown	1 cup packed	7 oz.
	2¼ cups packed	1 lb.
confectioners'	4½ cups sifted	1 lb.
granulated	2¼ cups	1 lb.
Walnuts, shelled, chopped	1 cup	4 oz.

Measuring Equivalents

3 teaspoons	1 tablespoon
4 tablespoons	¼ cup
8 tablespoons	½ cup
5 tablespoons + 1 teaspoon	⅓ cup
16 tablespoons	1 cup
1 liquid oz.	2 tablespoons
4 liquid oz.	½ cup
8 liquid oz.	1 cup
1 cup	½ pt.
2 cups	1 pt.
2 pts.	1 qt.
4 cups	1 qt.
4 qts.	1 gal.
1 lb.	16 oz.

Conversions Table

Weights

Ounces and Pounds	Metric Equivalents
¼ oz.	7 g.
⅓ oz.	10 g.
½ oz.	14 g.
1 oz.	28 g.
1¾ oz.	50 g.
2 oz.	57 g.
2⅔ oz.	75 g.
3 oz.	85 g.
3½ oz.	100 g.
4 oz. (¼ lb.)	114 g.
6 oz.	170 g.
8 oz. (½ lb.)	227 g.
9 oz.	250 g.
16 oz. (1 lb.)	464 g.

Temperatures

Degrees Fahrenheit	Degrees Centigrade or Celsius
32 (water freezes)	0.0
108 to 110 (warm)	42.0 to 43.0
140	60.0
203 (water simmers)	95.0
212 (water boils)	100.0
225 (very slow oven)	107.2
245	120.0
266	130.0
300 (slow oven)	149.0
350 (moderate oven)	177.0
375	191.0
400 (hot oven)	205.0
425	218.0
450	232.0
500 (very hot oven)	260.0

Liquid Measures

U.S. Spoons and Cups	Metric Equivalents
1 teaspoon	5 ml.
2 teaspoons	10 ml.
3 teaspoons (1 tablespoon)	15 ml.
3⅓ tablespoons	½ dl. (50 ml.)
¼ cup	60 ml.
⅓ cup	85 ml.
⅓ cup + 1 tablespoon	1 dl. (100 ml.)
1 cup	240 ml.
1 cup + 1¼ tablespoons	¼ l.
2 cups	480 ml.
2 cups + 2½ tablespoons	½ l.
4 cups	960 ml.
4⅓ cups	1 l. (1,000 ml.)

Appendix 2

Mail-Order Sources

American Spoon Foods
1668 Clarion Ave.
P.O. Box 566
Petoskey, MI 49770
(800) 222-5886
(616) 347-9030
Dried sour cherries, fruit preserves

Balducci's
424 Avenue of the Americas
New York, NY 10011
(212) 673-2600
(800) 822-1444
Catalog available
Specialty items

Birkett Mills
P.O. Box 440A,
Penn Yan, NY 14527
*Whole-grain flours, roasted buckwheat
(kasha)*

Bridge Kitchenware Corp.
214 East 52nd St.
New York, NY 10022
(212) 688-4220

Brookside Farm
Tunbridge, VT 05077
(888) 919-7673
Pure maple syrup

Brownville Mills
Box 145
Brownville, NE 68321
(402) 825-4131
(800) 305-7990
Stone-ground flours and grains

Burnt Cabins Grist Mill
P.O. Box 65
Burnt Cabins, PA 17215
(717) 987-3244
Flours and grains

The Chile Shop
109 E. Water St.
Santa Fe, NM 87501
(505) 983-6080
Catalog available
All chili products

Chukar Cherry Company
320 Wine Country Road
Prosser, WA 99350-0510
(800) 624-9544
(509) 786-2055
*Dried cherries, chutney, dessert sauces,
preserves*

Clearbrook Farms
3015 Kemper Rd.
Sharonville, OH 45241
(513) 771-2000
(800)222-9966
Fruit preserves, dessert sauces

Coombs Beaver Brook Sugarhouse
P.O. Box 503
Junction Rts. 9 & 100
Wilmington, VT 05363
(802) 368-2345
Maple sugar products

Dean & Deluca
560 Broadway
New York, NY 10012
(212) 226-6800
(800) 221-7714
Specialty items

Dundee Orchards
P.O. Box 327
Dundee, OR 97115
(503) 538-8105
Hazelnuts

El Molino
P.O. Box 2250
City of Industry, CA 91746
(877) 319-0360
Whole-wheat pastry flours, stone-ground natural-grain flours

Great Grains Milling Co.
P.O. Box 427
Scobey, MT 59263
(406) 783-5588
(800) 784-5589
Flours and grains

Great Valley Mills
1774 County Line Rd.
Barto, PA 19504
(800) 688-6455
Stone-ground flours and grains, butters, all-fruit preserves

Hazy Grove Nuts
P.O. Box 25753
Portland, OR 97225
(503) 598-9157
All variety of nuts available

Hoffritz
324 World Trade Center
New York, NY 10048
(212) 938-1936
Complete selection of cutlery

Kenyon Cornmeal Company
P.O. Box 221
21 Glenrock Rd.
West Kingston, RI 02892
(401) 783-4054
(800) 7-Kenyon
Flours, meals, miller's bran

King Arthur Flour Baker's Catalog
R.R. #2
Box 56
Norwich, VT 05055
(800) 827-6836
Complete selection of baking supplies

Kitchen

218 Eighth Ave.
New York, NY 10011
(212) 243-4433
(888) 468-4433
Dried chilies

Kitchen Glamor

39049 Webb Ct.
Westland, MI 48185-7606
(800) 641-1252
Cook's Tools Catalog
Complete selection of quality cooking and
baking equipment

La Cuisine Kitchenware

323 Cameron St.
Alexandria, VA 22314
(800) 521-1176
Complete selection of quality cooking and
baking equipment

M & S Produce

P.O. Box 220
Alcalde, NM 87511
(505) 852-4368
New Mexican products, blue cornmeal

Maid of Scandinavia

P.O. Box 39426
Edina, MN 55439
(800) 328-6722
(612) 943-1508
Baking supplies

Manganaro's

488 Ninth Ave.
New York, NY 10018
(212) 563-5331
(800) 472-5264
Wonderful New York source of Italian cheeses
and other products

Mariani Nut Company

P.O. Box 808
709 Dutton St.
Winters, CA 95694
(530) 795-3311
All variety of nuts available

Missouri Dandy Pantry

212 Hammons Dr. East
Stockton, MO 65785
(800) 872-6880
out of state (800) 872-6879
Black walnuts plus all variety of nuts

Moon Shine Trading Company

1250-A Harter Ave.
Woodland, CA 95776
(530) 668-0660
(800) 678-1226
Catalog available
Variety of natural sweeteners

New Hope Mills

R.D. #2
Box 269A
Moravia, NY 13118
(315) 497-0783
Flours and grains, syrups, honeys

Nunes Farms Almonds
P.O. Box 146
San Anselmo, CA 94960
(415) 459-7201

Oregon Apiaries
P.O. Box 1078
Newberg, OR 97132
(503) 538-8546
(800) 676-1078
Catalog available
Selection of honeys

Paradigm Chocolate Company
5775 SW Jean Rd.
Ste. 106A
Lake Oswego, OR 97035
(503) 636-4880
(800) 234-0250
Catalog available
Dessert sauces

The Peanut Patch
P.O. Box 186
Courtland, VA 23837
(757) 653-2028
(800) 544-0896
Catalog available
All peanut products

Pecos Valley Spice Company
c/o Savouries, Ltd.
1450 Heggen St.
Hudson, WI 54016
(715) 386-8832 Ext. 100
Blue cornmeal

Professional Cutlery Direct
(800) 859-6994
Great savings on the finest selection of
cutlery, cookware, and essential chef's tools

Rocky Top Farms
11486 Essex Rd.
Ellsworth, MI 49729
(616) 599-2251
(800) 862-9303
Catalog available
Fruit preserves, dessert sauces, fruit butters

Rowena's
758 West 22nd St.
Norfolk, VA 23517
(800) 627-8699
Jams and jellies (apricot ginger, carrot, berry,
peach, orange, clove)

Shiloh Farms
P.O. Box 97
Sulphur Springs, AR 72768
(501) 298-3297
(800) 362-6832
Flours and grains, natural sweeteners

The Spice House
1941 Central St.
Evanston, IL 60201
(847) 328-3711

Sunnyland Farms, Inc.
P.O. Box 8200
Albany, GA 31706
(912) 883-3085
(800) 999-2488
Catalog available
Black walnuts

Sur La Table
1765 Sixth Ave. South
Seattle, WA 98134-1608
(800) 243-0852
Excellent selection of cutlery, cookware, and other essential chef's tools

Timber Crest Farms
4791 Dry Creek Rd.
Healdsburg, CA 95448
(707) 433-8251
Dried fruits, dried tomatoes, almonds, pistachios

Todaro Brothers
555 Second Ave.
New York, NY 10016
(212) 532-0633
All manner of Italian ingredients

The Vermont Country Store
P.O. Box 3000
Manchester Center, VT 05255
(802) 362-2400
Pure maple syrup, maple butter

Walnut Acres Organic Farms
Penns Creek, PA 17862
(570) 837-0601
Flours, grains

White Lily Flour Company
Box 871
Knoxville, TN 37901
(800) 264-5459
An excellent source of soft wheat pastry flour

Williams-Sonoma
P.O. Box 7456
San Francisco, CA 94120
(800) 541-1262
Catalog available
Kitchen equipment and fine ingredients

Wood's Cider Mill
7482 Weathersfield Center Rd.
Springfield, VT 05156
(802) 263-5547
Cider jelly, maple syrup, cider syrup

Index

The Everything® Cookbook

Faith Jaycox, Sarah Jaycox, and Karen Lawson

Trade paperback, $12.95
ISBN: 1-58062-400-6

You don't need to be a world-class chef to cook delicious meals. *The Everything® Cookbook* contains over 500 simple, easy-to-follow recipes for dishes that are hearty, healthy, and perfect for today's hectic schedules. You'll learn how to serve scrumptious dinners to family and friends, make perfect breakfasts and brunches, create lovely desserts and snacks, and more! And the recipes are based on ingredients you probably already have. Whether you're cooking a dinner for two—or a feast for fifty—you'll learn how to create your favorite foods perfectly every time. Complete with definitions of cooking terms, and explanations of basic techniques and essential ingredients, *The Everything® Cookbook* really does have it all!